YOU CAN STOP

A smokEnder Approach to Quitting
Smoking and Sticking to It

JACQUELYN ROGERS

SIMON AND SCHUSTER   NEW YORK

ACKNOWLEDGMENTS

How can I possibly express my thanks to the thousands of wonderful people who have helped me gain knowledge, develop experience and guide my days so that I might be in a position to write this book? First I should thank all the smokers who have become smokEnders and have told me their stories; then all the fine people who have worked with me during the past eight years to help deliver the program; and finally, all those who actually propelled this book from concept to deadline.

I will hope that all who have shared our work and have made a contribution to my knowledge and effort will know that I am grateful and that I offer my sincere thanks.

And to those who helped with this book I want to express special thanks. To Harriet Pilpel for her gracious guidance; to Joanna Ekman for her patient support; to Barbara Davidson and Lois Rafalko for their talented assistance; to Ruth Strine for her diplomacy, scheduling wizardry and devotion; and to my editor, Alice Mayhew, whose expertise and professionalism were necessary and appreciated.

J. R.

DESIGNED BY ELIZABETH WOLL
MANUFACTURED IN THE UNITED STATES OF AMERICA

1   2   3   4   5   6   7   8   9   10

LIBRARY OF CONGRESS CATALOGING IN PUBLICATION DATA

Rogers, Jacquelyn.
    You can stop.
        1. Cigarette habit.   I. Title.   II. smokEnders, inc.
RC567.R64   362.2'9   77-15032
ISBN 0-671-22587-1

To my husband, Jon, for his love and unwavering support;

To our children, Joan, Jim, Lilla and Peter, for cheering me on and encouraging me to make my contribution.

Without them, I'd still be smoking.

PUBLISHER'S NOTE

With the development of smokEnders as both a movement and a business enterprise in 1969, Jacquelyn Rogers established what is today an international phenomenon. She and her husband, Jon, a practicing dentist, believed they could revolutionize the attitude toward smoking in this country by offering a truly effective means of quitting smoking which they had developed to "cure" Jackie of her twenty-two-year habit. They started on an ambitious campaign to develop both the health-care delivery system for their method and a consistently reliable means of providing it to the general public on a mass basis.

Now hailed by physicians and health agencies, the smokEnder method has stood the test of time. To this writing, over 100,000 smokers have entered the program, from coast to coast and in Canada and Norway; this supports the Rogerses' conviction that smokers would be anxious to quit if they knew how.

A wife and mother of four children, Jacquelyn Rogers began her study of the smoking problem shortly after she married in 1949. Her husband objected to her smoking, and she began to inquire informally into all the available quitting methods and techniques. Finally, in 1968, she prepared a formal research project that was designed to develop an effective method to free herself from her compulsive habit. This book is based on the central principle of smokEnders: you face in the right direction to quit smoking by careful preparation, by developing the right attitude and by knowing you're worth the benefits. It reflects Mrs. Rogers' knowledge and experience gained through ten years of working with smokers and a twenty-two-year history, which preceded it, of being a smoker and trying to quit. Mrs. Rogers moved from trial and error to analysis of the data and thus to the most successful method for stopping smoking yet devised.

contents

Publisher's Note   6

Introduction: The Miracle of the Human Mind   9

3 Getting to Know Yourself   15

4 Putting It All Together: How You Use
   Smoking to Protect Yourself—What to
   Do Instead   44

5 Learning How to Cope   57

6 Rationalizations   79

7 Cigarette Advertising: Reward Parodies   94

8 Changing Other Habits: What About
   Alcohol, Coke, Pepsi, Coffee and
   Marijuana?   102

9 Addiction   111

10 Rights   120

11 What Do You Say to Someone You Love
    Who Smokes?   135

12 HUNCHES ABOUT WHY PEOPLE SMOKE;
WHETHER SMOKERS ARE DIFFERENT; WHY
PEOPLE GO ON SMOKING 144
13 WHAT CAN MAKE YOU QUIT? 153
14 BENEFITS OF QUITTING 163
15 SUMMING UP: THINGS TO DO IF YOU'RE READY
TO QUIT 172
LAST WORD 184

introduction

THE MIRACLE OF
THE HUMAN MIND

When I was asked to write this book, I hesitated because I knew volumes have been written about smoking both in scientific literature and in the popular press. Books and articles about how to quit smoking; books and articles about the cost to the human body and to society.

But it occurred to me that no one ever talked *to* the smoker about the "bridge" between the time when he (read throughout, he or she, of course) first becomes aware of a negative aspect of smoking and the moment when he makes a conscious effort to quit.

So I'll try to cast some light on this large and frustrating national problem and at the same time give smokers some helpful insight into their own experience, in the belief that smokers *can* quit smoking—and that the act of quitting can be pleasant and give an individual a boost that can trigger off a success spiral in his life.

I understand so well the frustration with which health educators and the government view the efforts that have been made and the dollars that have been spent, all with such meager results. Smoking is on the rise, especially among young people.

It's exactly this frustration which causes serious people in health education to throw up their hands and say, "People just don't *want* to stop smoking; there's no point in spending any more time and effort."

I disagree with them. I'm a radical on the subject of teaching old dogs new tricks. I believe that people *can* stop smoking and that they would really *like* to stop smoking once they've changed their preconceived ideas—about smoking, about themselves, about what it means to quit. I also believe they would succeed in quitting if they had "all their ducks lined up" and approached the endeavor correctly. Not "intelligently," not "rationally." Just correctly.

There's no course in medical school that teaches doctors "Treatment for Stopping Smoking." There's been no practical approach to quitting which spells out changes in attitude and habit patterns that are necessary to even enter the quitting stage and to achieve the possibility of success.

That's why I'm writing this book. I hope that I can help you to bridge the gap between the point of discouragement and the point at which you finally, actually take your leap into the world of freedom from smoking.

I'll talk about the benefits of quitting smoking as a means of achieving a sense of personal freedom and rejuvenation. I'm not promising a new life—just a chance to improve the quality of your present life. More importantly—because quitting is an exercise in self-improvement, and self-mastery, that is very tangible, measurable—I promise that when you stop smoking you'll find it much easier to reach other goals and successes.

Somehow this works because of the miracle of the human mind: the more we use it and stretch it, the better it works and the more it expands. And because if success is achieved in one area of life, it carries over. I've been through all the hard schools. I tried all the techniques that were available at the time . . . I tried and tried, and failed and failed, until I realized that it was my own mind that was holding me back, and that only my own mind could help me succeed. In the process I thought about certain insights that eventually led to my smokEnder program.

During those discouraging and degrading twenty-two years of smoking and quitting, I wondered a great deal about smoking. What is the secret? Where's the key to the lock that has me bound to a habit which I desperately want to be free of? Is it a pleasure? Do I really enjoy it? Do I lack willpower? Can I ever be free of that horrible craving for a cigarette? How do I get out of this trap?

I suspected there was more to it than I had been told.

During my years of wonder—and my later years of studying the problem on a more scientific basis—I discovered what I had susupected: Smoking wasn't just a nasty little habit. It was far more complex than we smokers had ever been told. Indeed, it was an amalgam of a vast assortment of actions, reactions, attitudes, beliefs, emotional dependence and physiological addiction to a powerful drug. It was similar to the circuitry of a computer.

How was I to attack this hydra of a problem? I wanted to solve the puzzle—and more important, I wanted to free myself from the nagging, mind-consuming *craving* for a cigarette and walk away from it with a happy, comfortable feeling of indifference to smoking.

The quest was long and hard. And interesting. With many surprises.

The first surprise was that I did it. It worked. I'm free. With *no* traces of craving.

The second surprise was that I truly enjoy not-smoking. It's a pleasure I hadn't anticipated. I feel physcially and emotionally *free*. And I'm able to deal with day-to-day responsibilities with much more ease and control.

The third surprise was the discovery that the barrier to freedom was not the habit itself—which could easily be broken mechanically, as is done in the smokEnder program—but rather the aura of personal attitudes with which we surround ourselves as smokers: what we think of ourselves, how we deal with problems, how we cope with life, how we relate to others, how we use smoking in our search for satisfaction in life and how we lean on cigarettes to supplement our often distorted view of ourselves.

The fourth surprise was that I came to know myself a lot better. On a level that had eluded me all my adult life. I now know that my life has been put into focus. I'm comfortable with my existence. I accept myself as I am. It's my life, and I'm the boss of my life. That was a lot more than I had expected from just quitting smoking. All that I'd learned so hard is borne out by thousands of smokers who were eventually to tell me about the same suffering, the same physical and emotional weariness, the same rationalizations, the identical failures.

It's important to remember always that your problem is not unique. Tens of thousands who used to feel as you do now have succeeded. You can succeed too!

From having listened to those thousands of smokers, I can say with confidence that most smokers would like to quit but don't know how to *prepare* for it. There is a gigantic step that must be taken before they can approach the actual quitting. That critical step is the prequitting phase—the one prior to the actual effort. It takes certain careful preparation similar to preparation by an Olympic athlete for the big event. And most smokers are unaware of this step, so they enter the big event without any preparation. They go cold turkey and generally fail miserably. They were not in condition.

That's what this book is all about. It's the preconditioning step you need to get yourself into gear for quitting. It leads you through that important prequitting phase necessary for success.

But I'm not going to tell you to quit smoking—or harass you with the hazards of smoking. I believe smoking is very personal. If you want to smoke, I have no right to tell you to quit. That's your business. And I assume you're well informed and know the hazards, so I won't beat a dead horse.

The secret key I was looking for was that it was necessary to understand myself first—and to accept myself as a worthwhile human being—before I could *begin* to quit. That's what I want to share with you in this book: how to get ready to quit smoking. This isn't a classic How to Quit Smoking book, but it will probably do more to help you quit than any other book or device on the market.

This book will work to get you into gear—but you must work along with it. The undertaking should be fun as well as useful. At the very least you will gain some rich new insights into yourself, some new tools to cope with the problems of daily living; and perhaps best of all, you will attain a firm grasp on the kind of maturity that brings a sense of self-confidence, serenity and tranquillity.

So I hope both to transmit my enthusiasm for the pleasure of not-smoking and to give you some insights into your own smoking habits.

If I do no more than that, you'll benefit considerably because you'll be closer to quitting by a giant stride; if I help change your attitudes about quitting so that you really desire to take positive action and to succeed, as I believe you can, I'll be proud and gratified.

And if you've already quit smoking but want help to stay free, this book will help you with your emotional housekeeping so that you can handle stress; deal with problems; cope with life *without* reaching for a cigarette, pipe, cigar—or for that matter, candy, liquor or your fingernails. If this book provides you with reinforcement, I'll be pleased to have helped.

Most especially, this book is written to help you make a move toward a decision: either to continue to smoke without feeling out of control—or to begin your campaign to quit. And if you begin your campaign to quit, this book should help you believe in your ability to do it—with the result that you will learn to be nice to yourself. You deserve it.

And I assure you, it's worth it.

I hope you enjoy getting to know yourself—it's the best show on earth.

three

GETTING TO KNOW YOURSELF

No, you haven't overlooked Chapters One and Two. And we didn't forget them. We left them out.

In most volumes about stopping smoking—and other self-improvement books—the first two chapters recount the origins of the "problem" and the "historical record" of its "growth."

Fine if you're a student of history, politics, agriculture or sociology. But that's not why you're reading this book. You want to know how to get out of the trap you're in—not why you're in it.

So we skipped the business about the Indians smoking peace pipes, and Sir Walter Raleigh, and the impact of the tobacco trade on the Colonies. I shall also spare you a recitation of the health hazards as well as the raging controversy between the tobacco industry and the health agencies.

You're past that. You know that you should quit smoking, and yet you still smoke. You're a reasonable person. Why *don't* you quit smoking? Smoking isn't a reasonable option.

Another thing: You may have succumbed to the belief that you don't have enough willpower to quit. Well, I have good news for you. Assuming you have enough will to wake up and get going each morning with reasonable regularity, and to perform the hundreds of duties required of you each day, you have all the willpower you need. If you counter that it's a matter of degree, let's remind ourselves that there are eminent doctors and judges, policemen and firemen who have to have wills of iron and who smoke.

What's the answer?

I discovered that the problem of quitting smoking was more complex than just shedding a "nasty little habit," and that it required more than willpower, or drugs or a pep talk—or certainly plastic pacifiers and other gimmicks. Here's the clincher: You've stopped a few times, very likely—sometimes for a day or so, maybe even a couple of weeks. Sometimes you couldn't get past breakfast without a cigarette—and hundreds of times you've said to yourself before going to sleep, "Tomorrow (or soon) I'll quit smoking: I'm killing myself . . ."

When you did summon up enough emotional energy to quit, after thousands of promises—or because your next-door neighbor, a heavy smoker, learned that he had lung cancer—you quit. By whatever means you tried—and there are hundreds of possibilities —let us say, for the moment, you did quit. For a bit. But if you were the kind of smoker I was, you were very uncomfortable, obsessed with a longing for a cigarette. Soon, hours later, maybe even days or weeks, you caved in and found an excuse to start smoking again. (Or maybe you hung in and are still not smoking but are fighting with clenched teeth and white knuckled—what I call "working on gut power.")

Either way you are miserable. You may have stopped lighting up, but you haven't really changed anything about yourself. The conditions and your attitudes about smoking and about yourself are the same. Cigarettes are your trusted "old buddies"—always there when you need them; ready to make anything bearable, better.

You feel lousy without cigarettes. Since you probably don't know what it's like to be an adult nonsmoker (like most smokers, you probably started to smoke in your late adolescence), you can't depend upon feeling good as a normal state without cigarettes.

Probably the biggest condition that requires real change is your attitude about the naked act of quitting. If you haven't taken this step, or you have taken it incorrectly, you're afraid of it; you think it will hurt; you believe you're unable to quit. If, by some miracle, you ever quit, you can't imagine being able to function effectively without cigarettes. You avoid the thought altogether, except for those "once-in-a-whiles" when your sense of righteousness propels you to one more resolution to quit. But see, the manner in which you approach quitting is so negative that you couldn't get close to success if you were shot through a cannon. There's a law of nature, I believe, which has been expressed in thousands of ways, certainly since Moses. It goes something like this: If you think you can't, you can't. You're licked from the start.

Though you may have tried quitting, avoided lighting up for a period, unless *all* the game pieces were in place your chances of succumbing to another cigarette were predictable. Your smoking habit was in a dormant state. It was waiting to spring to life at the first crack in your will.

So let's get to the heart of the matter.

WHO ARE YOU?

Before you can take a cold, hard (but friendly) look at yourself, you must understand the need for personal honesty and intellectual honesty. It may be some time since you've thought about these things in terms of yourself. Here's a chance to exercise your mind and character without exposing yourself publicly.

The objective is to strip away the bull you've built up about yourself and try to get a glimpse of the real you. It's a terrific feeling, worth all the effort. Before you start, buy a notebook and then close yourself off from interruptions—give yourself a free hour or so to work.

Set down all the most important facts about yourself and your life. Try to look at yourself objectively: the trick is to describe yourself as if to a third person so that you are easily recognizable. You have to include vices and virtues without shame or modesty. (The notebook you use is your personal workbook; it's private. You're free to pour your heart out without fear of criticism. That's very important!)

First, describe your personal appearance:
    (the usual characteristics)
    Overall impression of appearance
    What do you consider to be your best physical features, and why?
    What do you consider to be your worst physical features, and why?

Now, in order to list your personal accomplishments, embarrassments, tragedies and talents, make a personal résumé.
    Date and place born.
    Elementary school:
        What do you remember as the most poignant experience—something you longed for, or treatment by the neighborhood bully, or a huge worry?
    Junior high and high school:
        Describe your "popularity."
        In what subjects did you excel?   Any awards received?
        Were you unmercifully self-critical of your looks, behavior, grades, accomplishments?
        When did you start to smoke?
        Describe the exact circumstances. Include names and descriptions of your peers and elders who were party to your first experimentations with cigarettes.
        What did smoking do for you, for your self-esteem?
        What physical effect did it cause at first?

College/Military service/Other interim vocations:
    Dates attended   Degrees/awards, etc.
    What qualifications have you as a result of any additional enterprise after high school?
    Are you satisfied with the results of your efforts?   Why?

Did you miss or ignore any opportunities during that period of your life which you regret now?   What and why?

Can you recapture or rebuild or buy any such lost opportunities?

If you could, which would you concentrate upon now, to bring you personal satisfaction?

Employment history:

(The usual listing . . .)

If you're presently employed, how did you happen to get where you are? Did the job fall on you or did you make it happen?

Is it in a field that interests you?

If not, what would interest you more?

Why aren't you engaged in that field now?

Do you have any plans to work in that direction?

Social relationships:

Who was your first date?

How old were you?

Your first love?

How old were you?

Did you/do you date seldom or frequently while in high school/college?

If seldom, was/is it really by choice?

Did you have many friends or a few?

Describe your *best* friends from childhood to the present.

Do they have anything in common?

Do you confide in them, or are you a very private person?

If you have a mate, are you satisfied with the relationship?

If so, why?

If not, what are the principal reasons for dissatisfaction?

Can you do anything to repair or correct the problems?

If so, why don't you?

If you work, what is your feeling about the majority of your business associates/co-workers? Friendly or aloof?

Do you consider one in particular a special friend?

Whom?

Why?

Do you report to him/her or does he/she report to you?

Do you consider anyone a particular "enemy" or impediment to your success/happiness?

Whom?

Why?

Does he/she report to you or you to him/her?

Can you do anything to improve the relationship?

If so, why haven't you done it?

What's your experience with neighbors?

Which most friendly?

Least friendly?

Describe worst incident.

Whose fault?

Family realities:

Mother: Describe her.

What did/do you like best about her?

Least?

Father: Describe him.

What did/do you like best about him?

Least?

Briefly describe your relationship with:

Sister(s)

Brother(s)

Grandparents

Aunts

Uncles

Close cousins

Mate

Children, if any, individually

Put a plus in front of those with whom you generally have a harmonious relationship; a minus sign to indicate a dissonant relationship.

Personal objectives:

Quickly glance over your life and remark on the first, the most

easily recalled, the most outstanding disappointment in your
life. Describe it.
What has been the greatest tragedy in your life?
What has been the greatest success?
What gave you the best ego satisfaction?
What gifts/talents/qualities do you have?
What keeps you from using them?

Now there's a good profile of you down on paper and after a
lot of thinking about yourself. Look at it and see if you can get
a sense of yourself. Maybe you have to convince yourself you're
worth studying. Until you're convinced, let me tell you, you are.
You're special. Certainly worth the investment of your time.

Let's go to the second step of this exercise.

Since you are the sum of your thoughts and experiences, you
can take the results from the first exercise and place the elements
on a scale to get a hook on this person you've come to take for
granted. Chances are, you will be surprised at what you find—and
probably pleasantly surprised. Most of us have covered ourselves
with a lot of layers to hide the raw and rough spots of awkward
adolescence. We had conned ourselves into believing everyone
else was "cool" and sophisticated; that we could skinny by with
connivances (like smoking) to make us appear more poised. And
somewhere along the line of growing up, we learned to make
excuses for ourselves—why we couldn't finish a job, or get an "A,"
or be on time—or get a promotion, or a raise. It was always
somebody else's fault that we didn't fulfill our responsibility. Or
maybe we were too smart for the task, or undereducated? Or the
wrong religion? Or too rich, or poor?

What has all this got to do with quitting smoking? Well,
central to quitting smoking is getting to know yourself, accepting
yourself and growing up that last little bit. That means you must
stop making excuses for yourself. You must learn to be intellectually honest.

Later we'll go into the typical defense/apology reactions we all use at one time or another to get us off a hot seat—when we light up a cigarette (or grab a chocolate)—but first here's an exercise to focus on the strengths and weaknesses which we call your Reaction Profile.

	FREQUENTLY	SOMETIMES	NEVER
1. Do you brag to others about your ability or performance when in your own mind-view you feel you don't measure up to your words?	—	—	—
2. Do you procrastinate and then take a defensive posture, blaming someone or something for your own lack?	—	—	—
3. Do you claim to be "expert" in some matters in which you have only a passing knowledge in order to impress someone higher up?	—	—	—
4. Do you feel sorry for yourself because "life is hard" and "others get all the breaks"?	—	—	—
5. Have you played the martyr to friends, relatives and co-workers in order to be the "good guy"— liked by all—because you feel somewhat unworthy and inadequate?	—	—	—
6. And how's your Hostility Level? Do you resent the imposition on your time by others, or interference with your plans, to the degree that you'd like to "walk away from the whole thing"—or slug somebody? (Including your parents or spouse or children or job . . .)	—	—	—
TOTAL	—	—	—

Review your answers. Four or more "Nevers" means you are really quite dishonest with yourself. Four or more "Frequentlys" says you're dishonest with others. Four or more "Sometimeses" puts you in the normal range with the rest of us.

Okay. That's *you*. What does it do for your smoking problem? *It fixes the first step* in your changing view of yourself—or your *changed behavior*, whichever you choose. Necessary, because you must stop making excuses for yourself. I can hear you ask, "What has that got to do with my smoking?" All the smokers I've worked with since I started smokEnders have asked the same thing. And here's the point:

As smokers, we use the cigarette for many reasons (which we'll discuss further in the book)—but one of the principal reasons is as an excuse for our inadequacy (or what we perceive to be inadequacy).

We have come to believe we must be super "cool," competent, composed in all circumstances. And we try to uphold that image at all costs; somehow, to most of us, the cigarette is used to stall, distract, interfere, impede or cushion the effect of our incompetence or inadequacy.

This view of the usefulness of the cigarette didn't just happen to us; it was branded on our minds when we were youngsters, and it is reinforced daily by the abundance of cleverly created cigarette ads. So we *use* cigarettes. If you agree with that much, let's expose the reasons to light so that we can deal with them. Here's how to go about it:

For the next three days, observe yourself each time you smoke. As you light up, consider the act in a detached manner and ask yourself, "Am I *using* this device of lighting up in some way?" You will find interesting answers, if you're honest with yourself. You may discover you're avoiding answering a question or getting on with your work; you may be seeking poise in a social encounter that causes you discomfort or anxiety; or you may be simply rewarding yourself after a particularly difficult (or boring) activity.

In the chapters to come, we'll discuss more specifically what each of these "uses" is and how you can deal with each without relying upon a cigarette.

So for the next three days, simply take a fresh, clear look at the possible uses. Get out your notebook, and every time you discover a new use you make of smoking, immediately write it down. That means you must carry the notebook with you at all times—if you're serious about getting to know yourself and getting a running start on quitting smoking. If you say that's inconvenient, let me remind you that you manage to carry packs of cigarettes around with you at all times—and that's mighty inconvenient, you know.

It has been said that one of the criteria of maturity is taking responsibility for your own behavior. I believe that is true—in particular in the matter of understanding the root of our "excess" use of cigarettes, food or alcohol. How does that apply to you? Think about it.

Now use the résumé you prepared to weigh your assets and liabilities—really your strengths and weaknesses—in order to gain a glimpse of your stock in trade. This analysis will provide a silhouette of you as a person. As the book proceeds, you will be given instructions to fill in the contours so that you can come as close as possible to seeing yourself as others see you—and then determine what you should do about it.

In your workbook, list your assets (talents, awards, experiences, education, position, pride items, etc., appearance as well as performance).

Then list your liabilities (weaknesses, inadequacies, appearance, behavior, shame items, etc.).

Sir Edmund Hillary, some people say, climbed 29,000-foot Mount Everest because it was "there." Who can argue with motivation? And who can define it? But that's what makes you tick, so you'd better find out what turns you on—and why you're what you are.

Every day you're motivated to accomplish many things—get a haircut, write a letter, pay a bill, go to work, stay home from work, go on a diet, call someone who owes you money, learn to ski, play tennis, study, dig a ditch, clean a toilet, write a poem. There are not always clear relationships between any of these actions. Why do you do them?

Psychologists tell us we have only a few natural motivators: self-preservation, ego, love, money, security . . . It's a given that self-preservation should be a strong motivator—and practically all humans are highly motivated to run like the devil to protect themselves if a man-eating beast comes charging at them. So many reasonable people (who don't smoke) assume that smokers will respond naturally to the life-threatening danger caused by smoking.

How stunned and bewildered they are when we continue to smoke in the face of horrible warnings. I've attended scientific meetings at which the principal topic was smoking and the treatment of smoking-induced illness where I've heard men of goodwill, medically trained, utter statements of righteous indignation regarding the mass of "unappreciative fools and oafs who are unwilling to quit smoking even though they know it's dangerous and hazardous."

Well, we're not fools and oafs because we go on smoking. (Although I don't, fortunately, smoke anymore, I still consider myself a smoker.) They underestimate the power of the cigarette habit and the weakness of the self-preservation motive in the face of the danger.

We smokers face many more dangers each day than the one we perceive smoking presents. We'd have to get inside a vacuum tube to avoid them. We risk our lives driving a car, riding elevators, eating, breathing, walking across the street—so, we reason, what's one more risk? Self-preservation, in the abstract, isn't quite the high-number motivator nonsmokers expect it to be. And neither is smoking quite the same manifestation of irrational behavior they assume it is. Therefore, acting rationally and stopping smoking for that reason just doesn't work for the majority of smokers:

Smoking is bad for me. Therefore, I will stop smoking. Baloney! It works in just the opposite way.

Here's what really happens. When a smoker is anxious or threatened by real or perceived danger, his first reaction is to reach for a cigarette. When the doctor tells you you're in the process of destroying your lungs or that your heart is coming loose, your most likely reaction is to reach for a cigarette. It's an ingrained defense mechanism against danger, worry, anxiety, threats, bad news—you name it. It's a comfort to an old-pro smoker who needs his faithful "old buddy" at a time like that.

What an intricate web of relationships! Unless you, a smoker, are informed about these bonds, your chances of breaking free are very slim.

So this book will help you recognize your response mechanism and give you some tricks, tools and techniques to cope—without resorting to a cigarette.

Now let's look at the rationalizations the ego provides when we evade self-preservation. We say (and we *all* seem to have invented this one ourselves, quite independently), "But I've got to die someday—of something. I might as well die happily with my cigarettes."

Another famous rationalization seems to be a piggyback to the first. "I don't necessarily believe all that cancer stuff. Really, nothing has been proved; the proofs are coincidence and not cause-and-effect, and if it were really catastrophic to smoke, the government would forbid the sale of cigarettes!" Which is another story in itself, and I'll discuss the politics of that issue in a later chapter, because, at the very least, it's as interesting as the latest nighttime soap opera.

And the third, and most classic, rationalization appears, as if to tie up the whole package with a tidy little knot: we smokers proclaim, "But it won't happen to me. It'll happen to the next guy." (This is the same defense we use against auto accidents and heart attacks.)

We build rationalizations and soon we don't know what we really feel. You know now that you've got to try to strip them away and get back to the basics of you—and what you *really* want—instead of what you have tricked yourself into thinking you want. It's easy, once you have some confidence that you can gain control over this monster habit.

Here's the first stroke in gaining confidence: Begin a list: *"Accomplishments I'm Proud of"* Sure it sounds corny, but wait until you begin to see the extent of the list, and discover the quantity and quality of successes you've had in dealing with formidable and complicated problems. We have a tendency to forget accomplishments—we seem to remember our failures; but in order to build confidence, you must build on your successes. A positive spirit comes from this, and that's what's essential if you really want to chuck smoking with grace and ease.

Here's your instruction:

For the next two weeks, continue to think of past successes. Write each of them in your notebook as you think of it—and elaborate somewhat, if you can. A good idea: dig out your old appointment calendars and correspondence files to aid your memory. The results will jolt you, perhaps, but that's good. What's important now is for you to get a good look at yourself from a distance.

Your list should begin to demonstrate that you *have* conquered difficulties and achieved a lot. As you translate that to stopping smoking, you will see, in black-and-white, that you can solve problems, follow instructions, climb high mountains, win races. An expanding list will produce a renewed sense of confidence in yourself and your ability to tackle smoking.

(If you are feeling poorly about yourself and can't find *anything* to start your list—here's one:

"I learned to tie my own shoelaces!"
—which is a pretty darned complicated thing to do when you
were probably only around 3 or 4 years old. Or review the résumé
you compiled. You'll find many accomplishments. And one thing
will lead to another.)

I could describe dozens of cases in which smokers couldn't
list any successes in their lives because they were obsessed
with their failure to quit smoking. They were overtaken by
hopelessness. A downward spiral of failure is pretty hard to
check by yourself. When you believe you can't accomplish
something, you won't. When you believe you can, you are
very likely to accomplish it.

I remember talking to the wife of the head of the department
of thoracic surgery in a prestigious London hospital. We met at
the World Conference on Smoking and Health in London, at
which her husband had been lecturing on the devastation
wrought by cigarette smoking and pleading with that august gath-
ering to take action to educate the public in order to prevent the
suffering he witnessed daily. He was very impressive. It was after
that session, as my husband and I were chatting with him about
smokEnders, that he introduced us to his wife.

Seated in the lobby of the building was a striking-looking
woman who had just lighted a cigarette. He beckoned to her. As
she approached, the doctor, with a blend of discomfort and de-
fiance, explained that he couldn't do anything with her about her
smoking. He felt it was hopeless, but even so, he wanted her to
meet us.

As we were being introduced, I watched the change in her
expression from cordial graciousness to defensiveness when she
learned we represented smokEnders. Predictably, she began the
famous liturgy of the smoker—as I had years before:

"But I enjoy smoking," she stated. "It's one of the few things
I do for my own pleasure. And furthermore," she added, "I'm
healthy as a tyke, so the chance of my being felled by one of
Charles's dreaded diseases is improbable. Not to worry, I tell him,

but he constantly begs me to swear off my simple pleasure.

"Sometimes I force him to admit that he's had patients with lung cancer who never smoked, which proves that smoking isn't the only cause of lung cancer. Why, this foul London air would probably cause cancer even if I quit smoking, so I might as well take my chances and die with my cigarettes."

Sound familiar?

Now let's get back to her confidence, or lack of it, and see how it leads to the development of motivation. Stand in her shoes for a moment.

Walking down the corridor to the restaurant, I asked her whether she had ever really tried to quit. It was after I had assured her that I understood how she felt, and that smoking was a very personal matter, and that I wouldn't attempt to tell her to quit. She relaxed her defenses considerably and confided to me that she had first tried to quit years before, by simply declaring that she would not consume any more cigarettes, after her husband had described the details of a particularly tragic case. The patient, an acquaintance, was the father of two young sons, one of whom attended the same school as their own son. The holder of a minor political office in their district, he was well known and well liked. He excelled in sports and was something of a local hero. He exuded good health and vitality. The time of the local marathon event was approaching when her husband, looking particularly drawn, told her that Phillip wouldn't be running the mile in that year's meet—or ever again—because he had just detected an advanced case of lung cancer. The most he could hope for was a few months.

The woman, even now, reciting the story, looked pained. "It seemed so unnecessary, and such a waste. Phillip was so vital, yet so suddenly debilitated. And then, just as suddenly, he was gone. It was terrifying.

"But the *most* terrifying aspect was that down deep inside me, I had the sense that Phillip had caused his own death, that it was self-destruction. So it was the horror of doing myself in, rather than the possibility of cancer, that caused me to vow to give up the habit."

And she described the familiar process of throwing away the pack of cigarettes on the spot, with all good intentions. She hadn't bargained for the unbelievable craving and obsessive desire for a cigarette. She couldn't concentrate on anything for very long. Her mind continually focused on the fact that she desperately wanted a cigarette. She felt cold and hot; stomach cramps alternated with nausea. Her disposition and patience hit an all-time low.

Recalling the experience now, she remarked that she was "as unprepared for the reaction as I was for labor and the delivery of my child." She commented that she had at least received something of value as a result of her labor, whereas the withdrawal experience had provided her with nothing except a loss of her self-respect.

She described how she had finally succumbed to her craving and bought a pack, which she consumed in short order. "And," she said, "right there and then I decided I'd never put myself through that agonizing, humiliating experience again."

I asked if she'd ever tried again, in spite of her pronouncement. She nodded, wearily. "Yes," she said, "Charles was at me regularly, and so from time to time I'd go through the motions of quitting. But I knew I couldn't really quit, and I dreaded the whole wretched effort. He certainly doesn't understand, and he has deliberately chosen to ignore my requests that he allow me to live my own life. He persists in reminding me that I shouldn't smoke and that it might very likely lead to serious lung problems.

"Lately we've been trying to ignore the problem, but every time he comments about my smoking, it seems to trigger me off to light up another. Seems like something perverse within me forces me to be obstinate."

I listened to her story with sadness and sympathy; it seemed so much like my own. But I had been luckier: I had a husband who had prodded me on to finding a means of freeing myself from the problem. So I clearly understood what she was feeling—and felt I could help her at least face in the right direction.

I thought about the situation and arrived at a few reasonable conclusions:

1. Her failures had destroyed her confidence in her ability to quit.
2. She feared the pain of withdrawal.
3. She hadn't the proper motivation to quit. It was obvious she was attempting to quit for her husband's sake—not for her own interest.
4. Her "rights" were being abused: since her husband had in fact ordered her to stop, her "right" to self-determination was threatened, and human nature caused her to react by defending her smoking posture.

She was defeated before she started. I suggested she try a different approach. First, I assured her, she *was* capable of quitting smoking if she could attain the three objectives necessary to overcome her mind-set.

She wanted to know what they were; but first, she wanted to know how I could be so sure she could quit smoking. I told her that from my experience with thousands of smokers—many who were much more emotionally and physically involved than she— I knew the signs which blocked success, and that when they were removed, even the most addicted smoker was freed.

She expressed a timid interest. I think she was half afraid I couldn't help her and half afraid I could.

Here are the keys I gave her:

First, she had to believe she *could* quit.

Second, she had to find an intensely personal reason—not just pleasing her husband—for wanting to quit and convince herself there was benefit in quitting (and in not-smoking).

Third, she really had to determine that she was worth it. This book is directed toward giving you those three keys.

MAKING PLANS, SETTING GOALS

Now let's make some plans and set some goals. For ideas of ways to change yourself—if you really want to—refer back to the questionnaire under "Who Are You?" In the personal-appearance section you were asked, among other things, "What do you consider to be your worst physical features?" Start with that. If your hair is too thin or too drab or unattractive, begin a list of ways to improve your hair. One might be investigating a wigmaker or a hairstylist. Ask people you meet who have attractive hair what they do, where they go, what they recommend for you. You'll learn a lot, because it's very likely they had some sort of problem and found a way to resolve it.

To illustrate the importance of doing something to improve your appearance in order to give yourself a boost, let me tell you about a smokEnder graduate I recently met at a conference with corporate executives who were interested in providing their employees with a means for quitting smoking. They had invited me to present the smokEnder approach because our graduate had fine things to say about the method. I hadn't seen him for about two years, and he had changed remarkably. I couldn't quite put my finger on what was different, but he had a certain bearing and presence that weren't part of my memory of him. In fact, my memory was of a rather colorless, self-effacing gentleman.

He told me about changes he had made in his life as a result of quitting smoking, lessons he'd learned from smokEnders that had helped him take hold of his life. It had given him the confidence to change many things in his life.

He followed a similar formula for stopping smoking and for developing other personal goals. I'll try to describe that phenomenon in this book. It's easy enough to tell someone to do something and that it will produce results. You have to be an active participant in your own "conversion."

That's what Greg McPherson told me that day. "Jackie, I heard what you said, but I couldn't convince myself, first of all, that I was able to direct my own life and secondly, that I was worth it." He talked about his feelings about himself then—feelings he now sees as "self-limiters." He'd lost respect for himself because he smoked even though he felt a heavy responsibility for his three young children and realized that if anything happened to him, they'd be in bad shape. He'd become bald young, and it had caused him self-consciousness and humiliation. He had been withdrawn in social groups, even though he'd felt he had a lot to contribute and had longed to express himself. He had always felt that he could and would achieve some level of real contribution in his field, metallurgy, but during the last dozen years he had been discouraged.

"So," he told me, "I tried it your way and it worked! First I made a list of those things I liked least about myself; then I separated out the changes that were physically and intellectually unattainable, such as being six feet tall instead of five feet eight and becoming a concert pianist when in fact I have never played the piano. But making the list was revealing. I spilled out a lot of dreams and wishes I had forgotten about.

"Then I put them in order of importance to me and gave them numbers. For the next several weeks I concentrated on each item —trying to think of ways to make a transition in my life.

"After a slow start, some ideas began to come. Just as you'd said, the mind is a muscle which gets stronger as you use it, but the difficulty is getting it revved up.

"Well, I realized that one of the biggest limiters I'd been carrying in my bag of excuses was that I was bald. And it became clear that it was one of the few things I could really do something about. I had always resisted thinking about a hairpiece, because I thought it was hokey. I told myself that if God had wanted me to have hair he wouldn't have made me bald and that wearing a hairpiece was sheer affectation. But I became aware of some top guys in my company who had quietly changed their appearance, without fanfare. They had 'lost' their baldness.

"Then I remembered the smokEnder advice to change those things you can and learn to cope with those things you can't or don't choose to. So I gave a lot of thought to whether what was inside that bald head was more or less important than what was outside it—and came to some exciting conclusions. It wasn't the hair that made me do a good job—or kept me from doing it. It was my perception of myself. But more than that, it was also my consciousness of the reaction of others to me/my baldness. I perceived they were less respectful of me than of others.

"Now that I have changed, Jackie, I'm not sure whether I was correct—whether others were less respectful of me because of my baldness or because I presented the image of inferiority and they responded to that; but this much I do know: when I got my hairpiece I began to feel better about myself, and I'm having a ball. It's like a new world for me. And I know my attitude has affected my relationships with others.

"I took a little kidding at first, but people soon forgot about it. When I met new people, they saw the confident me and responded. I've been promoted twice and expect that I'll soon be directing my own department, which is exactly where I'd like to be.

"And one day, I'll probably start going without my "bush," because I will have convinced myself that it's what's *in* my head that counts—not what's *on* it—and I will have developed the attitude of self-respect that comes from knowing you're good."

We all have self-limiters: we're too fat, too thin, too rich, too poor, too gauche, too smooth, too educated, not educated enough. And it's so convenient to use external conditions as excuses.

We can all grow and expand our abilities, contacts, knowledge, experience. What keeps us from trying? What makes some people take their lives in their hands and make something happen? We've got to want to make the effort to change because something excites us. That's motivation. So we all dream about something special.

In the next chapter we'll talk about what those "dreams" are and how you should rate them and sort out what you really want in life. But to conclude this mission of finding out what makes you tick, do this:

1. In addition to listing those things you like least about yourself, write down what you can do about improving them.

2. Write down missed opportunities you now regret. List those which you could make up for—studying business law, voice training, completing a degree or working in sales instead of accounting.

Choose one thing that excites you *and that is reasonably possible.*

Think of all possible ways you could move toward that goal. Write every idea you have about it in your book. This is how you create a plan, a map for your trip. Like a good sailor, you know which port you'd like to reach, but unless you have good charts, navigational equipment and a plan, the chances of reaching that port are very poor.

For instance, let's look at the case of a woman who called me recently to tell me her story. After spending the last eighteen years raising her family, she wanted to go back to the business world, which had interested her very much. She had found a good job as a records clerk for an importer before she entered the smokEnder program last year. The work was interesting, but her opportunities were limited because her French was very rusty. She realized she could move up if she could recapture her French skills. She regretted that she hadn't kept them up, because she had been a good student and had liked French in college, but she felt she was too old to do anything about it now and accepted the fact that she couldn't rise to the occasion.

Then, because she had stopped smoking, she had a burst of confidence. "If I could quit smoking, I can do almost anything," she said. (Don't we all!) And she had been told that quitting smoking should be a catalyst to other accomplishments. So she chose as her first goal after graduation from smokEnders getting back to her French.

"I called a friend in the language department at the local university and explained what I needed. He was delighted to discuss it with me. Actually, there were many possibilities, which surprised me."

She chose a crash-course seminar that could give her enough fluency to handle the first level of the new job. Her employer was delighted that she had made an effort to improve her ability to serve the company, and he worked out a training schedule which included additional courses at company expense.

She called to thank us for giving her the confidence she had needed to turn herself on. Of course, it was her own motivation that had done the trick.

3. List your "prime motivators"—those things which you really like to do, which you get excited about and are never too tired or too poor to do: going to the theater or a football game; having your hair cut; shopping for antiques; working out at the health club; painting; reading porno; comparing this year's sales with last year's; going out for dinner; having friends in for dinner; writing poetry or a procedures manual.

Psychologists tell us we can know the person by his past performance. You are the sum total of all your thoughts and actions to this point in your life. So if you want to know what turns you on, look at what you have done so far. Why do you pick yourself up from a sickbed to join the gang at a political rally? Is it duty —or simply that you want to be there? When you find enough of the want-to's, you'll begin to see a pattern. You will probably learn that one of the prime motivators is *your* particular thing. Is it Ego? Love? Security? Self-preservation? Money? None of these is right or wrong. They simply cause people to do remarkable and sometimes impossible things—like climbing Mount Everest.

This exercise will help you in several ways: you'll get some insight into your real self; you'll have a better idea of which motivator will propel you toward deciding to quit smoking; it will give you some ideas of other ways to achieve satisfactions in your life. We all search for greater self-realization, because we all know instinctively there's more to us than we've had an opportunity to express so far, our undeveloped potential. Get on with it! It's your life. Make the most of it, with a plan and confidence that you can succeed.

4. List details of "my dream look." Plan to spend about one quiet hour this week thinking deeply about yourself.

If you could look any way you'd like, what would that be? Write it down. Describe all the aspects of that look. Head to toe. Size, weight, color, sex, type of appearance (rugged, fragile, pretty, chic, wholesome . . .)

Next check it against your appearance. What is it that makes the difference between you and your model? Why is that model more appealing to you than the way you are? Can you do something to come closer to your ideal? If you are, in your own eyes, an unsophisticated bumpkin and you want a new image, can you work out a staged transformation of your wardrobe, your hairstyle, your posture and other externals? I should caution, however, that you may be disappointed when you've changed. Or you may be pleased. But before you decide to change into somebody else, it's important to take the next step toward self-knowledge.

When you started smoking you may have wanted to emulate someone who seemed attractive. Can you recall the "look"? Is that look/style/manner similar to the one you described on the checklist above of your "dream look"?

It's important that you become extremely critical now of your inbred attitudes about what you think you want and what you really want. How important is that "look" now? What residual ideas have you from the past? Think about that—a lot. If you're still hung up on people or ideas from ten years ago, you have some more growing up to do. Pause now, and reflect.

Here's the relationship between this concept and getting around to quitting smoking: before you can throw away the crutch that made you look older, more sophisticated, "in," "cool" and all things beautiful, you've got to decide what was so damned important about looking and acting like that.

To help you focus on what you really appreciate in people, let's explore present and future models:

5. Make a list of those few people you most admire—in any and all walks of life. Think of people you know. Then scan the world to remind yourself of persons in world affairs, government, theater, medicine, law, business, society, education, art, dance, literature—anyone who has captured your admiration by his or her performance, contribution, even appearance. Next to each name, note what you admire about him or her. Study the list. It will be revealing. Then compare it with your dream model. I predict that you will be surprised. Most of us have changed. So keep up with your own tastes—and aim yourself toward your real desires, rather than the outdated ones.

This is a double task: you have to look from a smoker's point of view and from an adult's. If you started smoking for the same reasons as most of us—to be accepted by the gang and to appear more grown up more quickly—now is the time to see what you're carrying along that still works as a useful motivator. Do you still want to be accepted by "the gang"? Not likely. Do you still want to appear more grown up? Not likely. In fact, don't you really admire independence and individualism now? Don't you do some things just to be different? Perhaps the original reason for smoking is no longer useful to you? Yes, I'd say that was true of most of us.

Instead of wanting to appear more grown up, aren't you now a little concerned about your age—and how time is rushing by? Is that another reason for smoking which is no longer valid? I'd say yes to that one, too.

The next step in analyzing your relationship to cigarettes and the smoking habit is to find out where you're going now that you've broken with the past. But before you start the next chapter, please review your work requirements in this chapter, especially to get a firm grasp on your *new* model.

WHAT ARE YOU GOING TO BE WHEN YOU GROW UP?

Remember how when you were a kid that question was the center of your world? Unless you are in the midst of your education or a career change of your own design, think about what you want to be doing ten years from now.

Ask yourself: Do I like what I'm doing? Is it an end in itself, or a means to an end? What would I like to do eventually? Is it in addition to what I'm doing, or instead of? Am I often bored and restless? Is it at my job or at other times? Now that I have some job experience in one or several fields under my belt, what have I learned about the kind of job, the environment, the lifestyle, the demands on my time, my capabilities, my weaknesses, what bores me, what excites me?

Here's what all this is getting at. Too many smokers are unhappy with their jobs. It shows up in their smoking patterns. Before arriving at their store, office or plant, they smoke a lot. When they're asked about it, it often appears that they hate getting down to the responsibility or the hassle or the conditions of their job—and they smoke to stall the inevitable or to fortify themselves.

Once aware of this, they have been helped to eliminate this excess smoking, at least. In some cases, people change their routine to avoid what they most dislike about entering the workday. One man described his solution with a great deal of jovial satisfaction. He said he had discovered he hated to walk in the front door to his office each morning because a very cranky receptionist seemed to have saved up the worst problem calls for his arrival, and she would attack him with them in rapid-fire order, along with a bit of editorializing calculated to freeze his heart in terror and panic.

"She was a dependable, efficient person," he said, "and we weren't about to dismiss her. And there were no other positions open suitable to her skills. So I had to make the best of it."

He worked out a plan, according to his smokEnder instructions, to identify and then "repattern" any conditions that caused him to smoke excessively. "It was like playing a game of chess," he said. "I had to think of all the possibilities and risks, and find the best way to move ahead without making things worse."

Some of the options he considered were: Quit. Sneak in a back door. Come an hour and a half earlier. (She arrived an hour before the office officially opened.) Have the relief receptionist start the morning and allow the regular woman to come in later. Put in a request for a sales job instead of administration. Talk to her about the problem. Change the routine.

He decided to confront the problem face to face. He spoke to the woman and told her that he had a lot of important things on his mind when he came in each morning and that he wanted to unload those before he started on new ones. He asked her to collect all his calls and give them to him a half hour after he arrived.

She didn't become more gentle or more gracious, but she did as he'd asked. He had time to put his head together each morning. The mere act of walking into his office no longer mangled his spirit for the day.

There's an exciting postscript to this case. Several years later he told me he had, in fact, always wanted to get into sales, and the exercise in solving the problem of the receptionist had reminded him that one of his ambitions was to be a successful salesman. He was proud to tell me that he's now head of a sales group which deals in international commodities. He put his administrative experience together with his German and his desire to sell, and approached the vice-president in charge of international sales. After a trial period, he was given a territory, and after eighteen months he was put in charge of his group. He's a happy man, proud of himself. "I know it sounds like an exaggeration," he said, "but I really believe I was able to move ahead because I quit smoking: it gave me the knowledge of myself and the confidence I might never have achieved."

What can *you* do to live up to your potential? *You own yourself. Everything you say or do is yours.* You may make some mistakes along the way, and you may be ashamed of some of the things you've said or done. But you can often put those things aside and say, "Well, I learned something from that goof." Or, "Now it's time for me to take myself by the seat of my pants and push myself upward, instead of standing here wishing and whining about it."

First you have to decide what you want to do that you aren't doing (always within reason). Homemakers with small children may feel burdened and limited because they have little time for themselves. Business people say they are always rushed and haven't enough time to do things at home. Until we recognize what and where we are—and where we are is exactly "where it's at," in the parlance of the street existentialists—we might spend a lot of life waiting for something to happen. And while we're waiting we can do a lot of smoking . . . because somehow the two go together. See if there is evidence in your questionnaire of self-pity, for instance; or boredom.

If you really want to quit smoking, and get a bonus from it, here's your next exercise. Decide what you really want to do and be. Set your goals for the short term, intermediate term and long term.

Say to yourself, "Within the next year, I want to do/accomplish/gain/complete/learn/earn/lose/find/establish or otherwise achieve (whatever you dream of) in each of the following categories." Then repeat the drill, but say "Within the next ten years, I want to . . ." Then, one more time, ask yourself what the pinnacle of your life should be, in each category.

It will encourage you to know that a great many successful people use this or a similar technique to plot their goals in life. You aren't bound by any contract, and you can change your mind along the way. But this much is true: the chances are very good that you will achieve most of your objectives, once you have stated

	Within 1 Year	Within 10 Years	Ultimate Goal
Physically (Appearance)			
Vocationally (Job/Profession)			
Educationally			
Socially			
Financially			
Of/for family			
Sports			
Hobbies			
Of/for community			
Health			
Other _____			

them and cranked them into your dream system. You know that old baloney about "Anything the mind can perceive it can achieve"? Well, it's not baloney. It's true.

So think carefully. Dream and wish, and write down what you realistically hope to achieve with your life.

It's a good idea to date your entries and review the list frequently. Also, crank into your annual routine a time to recast the list—around New Year's, or your birthday, perhaps—to modify, to check off the things you've accomplished. What satisfaction! Each year you'll decide on your new goals for the short term. The fact that you will have achieved a number of your goals during the past year will inspire you to greater ambitions. There's nothing like an upward spiral. Nothing succeeds like success.

It's hard to say what we really want to do or be. There's so much to choose from. So for a starting point, begin a list of what you *don't* want to be. List all your distastes in all kinds of areas of activity, including house and home, educational disciplines, tasks, sports, social experiences, ways of travel—anything that you don't like and wouldn't like to have to do as a major part of your life. Add to this list every time you observe another dislike. From the growing list, you'll soon see the nature of your interests and what excites you, and you'll be wiser in setting goals for the future.

What has this all to do with quitting smoking? Plenty. First of all, if you reduce the level of frustration in your life, you have less need to smoke; less quick-on-the-draw reaching for a cigarette when you feel sorry for yourself. Second, if your days are spent doing things that give you a sense of fulfillment and you have a genuine feeling of respect for yourself, you eliminate several causes for smoking or for resuming smoking. Wind yourself up and go.

four

PUTTING IT ALL TOGETHER: HOW YOU USE SMOKING TO PROTECT YOURSELF— WHAT TO DO INSTEAD

Stop and think for a moment about how you use cigarettes. Let's run through a day with a typical smoker. I've prepared a composite smoker from the collection of data in the smokEnder files.

Meet Robert Sanderson of Cleveland. He's an attractive, successful vice-president of a large electronics concern. At 43, he can boast of most of the usual measures of success—house, car, boat, ski lodge in Colorado. He's devoted to his wife and three children. On the down side, his wife is changing her life-style by returning to school and working part time in a nearby pharmaceutical firm as a beginning lab assistant. Her work absorbs her; her attention to home and family is reduced. As a result, Bob has to attend to many family matters. Visits to the orthodontist, or to college campuses with the oldest child, have now fallen upon him. His already busy schedule has had to be rearranged to accommodate additional responsibilities. Also, his mother is becoming increasingly less able to care for herself because of Parkinson's disease, and he is distressed at leaving her alone. It's clear to him that the only real option is to have her come to Cleveland—and live with his family. But that has its obvious drawbacks.

Now let's run through a day with Bob and observe how he uses cigarettes.

The alarm goes off, the radio goes on. Before he's fully awake, Bob reaches for a cigarette on his night table and fumbles for his lighter. This is routine since college days, so it's now an ingrained conditioned response. If he thought about it he'd say, "I can't get going without a cigarette." Translated, that reads: "My body needs a shot of nicotine to get my adrenaline going; I'm sluggish and I need help." In some cases, it also reads: "I can't face the day—so I'll call upon my friend to stave off the dangers that lie ahead." So Bob lights up and drowsily considers the day and what faces him.

Soon he's shaving, aided by the ritual of the cigarette. It seems to make the shaving easier. If he watched the ritual, he'd roar with laughter at the sight of a grown man trying to scrape whiskers off his face while juggling to keep his cigarette dry and the smoke out of his eyes—squinting and cocking his head and drying his cigarette-holding fingers. He would see himself as a clown performing a ridiculous antic. If our Bob were Betsy, it would be a similar picture—except that she'd be trying to apply her makeup and juggle a cigarette at the same time. For Betsy, the humor is in the act of doing anything with her eyes—makeup or contact lenses. It's tough when you're squinting—especially if the cigarette is dangling in your mouth because you can't put it down on the wet sink!

Now Bob is ready for breakfast, which until recently was waiting for him. Since Natalie is rushed in the morning too, Bob pitches in to find the cereal for the kids. Oops—none left. Must go to the store. How about eggs this morning, children? No, you can't have pizza for breakfast. Natalie! Why the hell can't we keep a supply of cereal in this house? . . . No, it wasn't my turn to go to the store. . . . You knew I had to go to Chicago on Tuesday. . . . Yes, I know that was the day of your finals. . . . Natalie, can't we find some kind of housekeeper? . . . Cost be damned. . . . Yes, I know Robbie is going off to college next year and Mother will likely come to live with us. . . . No, I don't want to keep you from having a life of your own. . . . Here, let me get

the coffee ready while you finish making the kids' lunches. . . .
Where are my cigarettes?

And so it goes. Bob has his hands full coping with little problems—and larger problems caused by little problems—so he
reaches for a cigarette, which steadies him—or, at the very least,
relieves the tension.

Translated, that reads: I'm uncomfortable. I can't deal with
this situation and it causes me to be tense. I believe cigarettes
relieve my discomfort somehow, so lighting up will somehow
cause these problems to disappear. Bob also uses cigarettes to
protect himself from problems—and perhaps as an escape valve.
Really, he's creating bigger problems for himself, because the
nicotine makes him more edgy and tense. It's a matter of chemistry.

A stop in the bathroom before leaving for work. Bob believes
smoking is an aid to regularity and has convinced himself he
would become constipated if he didn't have a cigarette while he
was on the pot or just before entering the bathroom. Another
well-entrenched ritual. Of course it's not necessary to have a
cigarette in order to move one's bowels; it's just that Bob's body
has become accustomed to expecting the shock caused by nicotine to activate his digestive tract. Once he stops smoking, his
body will return to its natural manner of housekeeping.

He grabs his coat and the grocery list and dashes to the car.
Reaching for the keys, he reaches for his cigarettes. It has become
a requirement; somehow the ignition key won't work unless he
first lights a cigarette. This is a very subtle means of using a
cigarette. It's what we call in smokEnders a "hidden trigger." It's
one of the reasons Bob checks his pockets on leaving the house,
to be certain he has enough cigarettes to get him and his car
going. (If he used the bus or train, he'd light a cigarette to hasten
its arrival.)

In slightly more than an hour since Bob woke up he has used
five or six cigarettes: one to help him get going; one to help him
shave; one to help him get through the uncomfortable jumble of

the breakfast routine; one or two with coffee; one as an aid to regularity and one to get his car going.

Certainly all this could be called "habit"; but if you want to free yourself of the smoking problem, you'll gain by observing how you use cigarettes—so that you can change your attitude and therefore your dependence.

At the office, before he can get started, Bob lights up. Frequently, if he doesn't really like what he has to do, he lights up before getting to his desk—and stalls around doing other things until the cigarette is finished. In fact, almost anytime Bob wants to procrastinate, he lights up. It seems a very acceptable means of putting off the task at hand—and nobody can accuse him of goofing off. He uses his cigarette as a stalling device.

As he goes through his mail, he needs to think—and so he lights up again. He has come to associate his ability to "think" —concentrate—with the power of a cigarette. In fact, he is sometimes unable to "think" if he's run out of cigarettes—which convinces him that cigarettes *are* his ability to think. This is learned behavior at its starkest. Here's how to read it: Bob wants to think through a problem. Because of a well-practiced association of "sitting back and lighting up" in that situation, and also because the nicotine level soon drops in Bob's bloodstream if he doesn't light up, he would soon find himself squirming around in search of a cigarette so that he really would be unable to concentrate. It's not the cigarette which gives him the ability to concentrate, it's the lack of one that keeps him from it! (Until Bob has trained himself to recognize these situations and is no longer dependent upon nicotine, he *will* need to smoke to concentrate. Once free of the habit, he'll be able to concentrate more efficiently. Incidentally, his ability to think creatively is limited by the carbon monoxide and other gases he inhales in addition to the nicotine. They deprive the brain of oxygen.)

The phone rings. Automatically, Bob reaches for a cigarette. (Sometimes he has one already lit, resting in the ashtray, but the phone signals a cigarette, just as Dr. Pavlov's dogs learned to salivate when the bell rang signaling food. We smokers are conditioned to light up at the sight or sound or smell of certain triggers.) A tribute to our intellectual capacity: we can learn by means of repetition. Bob isn't really using a cigarette. He's just acting mindlessly.

If he's expecting a "bad news" call, he will continue to light up until it rings. In that case, he's using his cigarettes to ward off bad news and to protect himself from difficulties.

Sometimes we feel that a cigarette will make us strong and tough. So we anticipate a "bad news" call or visit with a couple of them wolfed down. This, in fact, is one of the reasons the cigarette ad with the cowboy and the horse works so well: People are afraid of appearing vulnerable and weak in the face of a stern situation. They think if they smoke cigarettes—and that brand in particular—they will seem as tough as that cowboy.

Bob goes to the Executive Committee meeting, worried about his project and the opposition of the chairman. A few cigarettes on the way with some coffee or a Coke, and another as soon as he sits down at the conference table. Whether he makes his point or not, Bob is using a lot of cigarettes to be tough and to relieve tension and discomfort. It's really a contradictory situation, of course, because toughness calls for heightened psychic tension— and calmness requires relaxed psychic tension! Bob is using his cigarettes at cross-purposes. (The truth is, he has by this time shot so much nicotine and carbon monoxide into his system, he's wound up like a mainspring—and the chances are he can be neither tough nor cool. Just jittery. In a later chapter, I'll talk about the physical effects of all these drugs and gases and the reasons they don't and can't do what the ads promise.)

If he makes his point, Bob lights up again to celebrate. If he loses his point, he lights up to soothe his bruised sensitivities. Now cigarettes are an act of reward or self-pity. Poor me, he says, in the latter case, I must do something nice for myself. I worked hard to prepare that project, the boss just doesn't appreciate me, I'll have a cigarette and make it a bit better. (This same attitude moves into and out of all our lives in varying degrees. A woman may feel sorry for herself because no one recognizes how hard she works to keep the house beautiful, or to make a splendid meal, or how she's always the last person to leave the office. A student may be disappointed in the response he receives from his teacher regarding a paper he worked hard at researching; a beautician may suffer a moment of self-pity if his client doesn't respond with a special comment of praise for the effort; and so on.) So Bob reaches for a cigarette instead of dealing with his feelings. After he has learned to live comfortably without cigarettes, he will deal with his feelings and his previous "treatment" of them.

There was another undercurrent at the meeting that had made Bob uncomfortable. He was the only one smoking. This was new. Several of the others had been heavy smokers. Now, the only smoker, he was self-conscious each time he lit up, but he was also very uncomfortable if he didn't smoke. (His friend Alex confessed he had felt the same thing in his car pool when he'd been the last smoker. The guys would make a fuss about opening the windows, choking, suggesting he could wait another twenty minutes until he was dropped off. And he was uncomfortable if he couldn't smoke during the trip. That was one of the reasons he finally quit.)

After the meeting, which was inconclusive and frustrating, Bob and Ted, who had supported his project, went to lunch to rehash. Ted was irked that Bob hadn't come fully prepared with the charts they had talked about when they had planned the presentation. Bob tried to convince Ted that he thought Ted had written the charts out of the plan, but Bob knew he was filibustering— and he recognized his "buck passing" as a cover for his procrastination. With all the problems at home, he hadn't gotten around to doing the charts they'd discussed the last week, although he had known when he promised to do them that he wouldn't have enough time. Now, recognizing his own intellectual dishonesty, he squirms inside and lights up. He's using cigarettes to relieve his emotional discomfort. Their drinks come, and he automatically has another cigarette. That one is pure conditioned response. After lunch, coffee and another cigarette.

The discussion turns to bringing in Guy Baker, an engineer in the design group, to work on improving the project. Bob isn't having any of that. Guy is light-years away from understanding the approach Bob believes is essential to success in this project. Besides, though he doesn't want to admit it, Bob has been worried about Guy moving up so fast in his department. He feels threatened. So he uses another cigarette to subdue his anxiety. Ted insists on bringing Guy into the project to give it the best shot he can. "So far, Bob, you haven't been able to sell it your way!"

Bob is outraged. Another cigarette. He begins a series of arguments and excuses to defend his efforts: he could have done it right from the start if Ted had budgeted it correctly, instead of pulling out the allocation for research into the GXH system. Both men are frustrated, so their anger finds easy breeding grounds.

Many cigarettes later, Bob returns to the office to plow through his work load. His mind isn't too clear: not only is he drowsy from lunch and the drink; he's reviewing the argument in his mind and thinking of "I-should-have-saids."

As his anger wears off, self-pity begins to enter. "Ted has no idea how hard I worked to put together that presentation. He didn't say one good word about it. He just carped about what I didn't do. Just because we didn't get a positive decision today, he's sore and blaming me. Poor me. I don't deserve this abuse. . . ." And he lights up. Now Bob is using cigarettes for one of the most common uses, self-pity. Somehow, subconsciously, he thinks/we think a cigarette will salve our wounds; put a Band-Aid on our injured emotions; "make it all better."

By four-thirty, two coffee breaks later, Bob has had several more cigarettes. He's feeling weary. He must finish the report he's working on, but he needs a lift—so he lights up. And he gets a lift, all right. For a short moment. Then he sags again, and lights up again. He's using cigarettes to pick himself up physically.

Pretty soon, he's so wound up, with all that coffee and nicotine, that he feels shaky. Leaving the office, he lights up to calm himself down. He takes a deep drag on the way out and tells himself it'll relax him. Now, it appears, he's using cigarettes as a relaxant.

If Bob stopped to think, he'd be surprised at his expectations —contradictory and unreasonable. How can he reasonably expect to have something pick him up and also calm him down?

This evening, on the way to the train, Bob stops at the friendly little bar near the station and buys two cans of beer—a trick he learned from his friend Tom, a lawyer who commutes. This way he can catch the earlier train, instead of taking time at a bar for the drink he so enjoys. And on the trip home, he can relax with a few cigarettes and a couple of beers. It would be fine, except that each night he brings home his briefcase with some work he had hoped to review on the train. So he promises himself, "I'll do it tonight after the kids go to bed, instead of watching TV."

At his station, he lights a cigarette as he walks to his car—or, if he was lucky enough to find a parking spot close to the station, he lights up as he reaches for his keys.

At home, instead of the calm orderliness he had hoped for, he is met at the sidewalk by Robbie, in his Scout uniform. Panicked. "Daddy, tonight's the Blue and Gold dinner—you promised you'd be home early—and Mommy said you'd remember to pick up the chocolate cake at Mrs. Eliason's on your way home from the station—because we promised we'd bring some dessert—all the guys bring stuff—and Mommy said she'd meet us there later, after her class . . . And now we're going to be late—and Mr. Paulis says a Boy Scout shouldn't ever be late . . . and . . . and . . ."

Usually when Bob comes home from the office, at least he can kick off his shoes and take off his jacket and have a drink as he pitches in to help get dinner, help with homework, clean up and get schedules sorted out. That usually means a cigarette with the drink before dinner. Maybe one or two more, and another during dinner; then two with coffee.

This evening, like most other evenings when he and Natalie are not entertaining or being entertained, is a frenzy of trying to get everyone and everything put back together again. Help the middle child with algebra; fix a stuck window; remember to get a button put back on a jacket; call Mother—didn't receive a letter from her this week, and forgot to send her one last week!; review the reports he meant to look at on the train. Whose turn is it to pack lunches?; who put Robbie's new red sweat pants into the washer with the white things?; I forgot tonight was the board meeting at the church and I promised I would be there.

In between and during the evening's comings and goings, cigarettes are used. Frustration, anger, weariness, joy, social exchanges, stalling simply from the habit of reaching for the pack because it is there!

Later in the evening, Natalie and Bob have a chance to relax together and watch TV. That's another smoking ritual perfected. It's so automatic Bob doesn't miss a moment of viewing as he reaches for the pack and matches. He lights up and returns the pack and matches to the exact spot on the chairside table for the next time. Generally he complains because "there's never anything good on TV anymore." Bored, he smokes more.

The most elaborate ritual comes at the end of the day. The last cigarette before bed is a very conscious one in Bob's routine. After a bedtime snack and cigarette, he washes and brushes his teeth, gets into bed with Johnny Carson on TV and lights up. The timing of this last cigarette is exquisite. It should be finished just as a commercial comes on, or else Bob lights up another cigarette to finish watching an act that has caught his fancy. But the last cigarette must be stubbed out just as the TV is turned off. It is almost a religious ceremony—paying respect to the God of the Night; expressing the need to formalize the close of day; a ritualistic preparation to ensure the coming of the new day. Most of us who smoke have this routine, except that some of us brush our teeth *after* the last cigarette instead of before.

So Bob turns off the lights and goes to sleep. Or maybe he goes to Natalie. If he does, he's bound to need a cigarette after sex. No one seems to know why this is a "trigger" for a cigarette for a great number of us. Perhaps, for Bob, it's a carry-over from his younger days, when he was told that that was what was done.

Around two or three o'clock in the morning, Bob awakens; reaches for a cigarette and sleepily lights up; wanders into the bathroom, in response to what he believes has awakened him; finishes his cigarette and returns to bed. And then he starts the whole process over again in the morning!

Are you weary and beat-up for Bob? So is he, but he won't know how much until he stops smoking.

Bob has used smoking as a propellant, a stalling device, a protection against "devils," a comfort in trying times, a lift, to calm down, to complete a pleasurable cycle, to relieve physical and social discomforts.

Throughout the book, you'll find answers to how to deal with many of those situations without cigarettes. You will benefit from the suggestions—but before you can apply them to your own situations, you must first determine how *you* use cigarettes and smoking.

So your next exercise is to take a quiet half hour and write your own "case history" of a typical day and figure out how you use cigarettes. You can refer to Bob's routine; surely some of his experiences must parallel yours. Some of your own are unique.

Be honest with yourself. Write down what you really do and feel, rather than what you wish you did and felt. The notebook you've been using is your workbook—no one else should have access to it—so you should have no doubts about writing freely and openly. You're not going to be criticized or judged.

You'll be asked in later chapters to think about your feelings and thoughts about smoking.

You've seen how most of us use cigarettes. You've analyzed your own uses. If you've done a thorough job of observing and reflecting on your "connectors" to the habit, you have moved strongly toward freedom.

Some of Bob's uses are obvious and some are rather more subtle. Here's a list to compare with your list. Do you smoke—

To get going physically in the morning?

To "ward off" threatening problems each day presents?

Automatically, without realizing you're lighting up (while shaving-/applying makeup; reaching for the ignition key; with coffee; using the telephone; with a drink; coming out of the theater; while typing, ironing, playing cards, for instance)?

To deal with situations that cause tension/anxiety/pressure/confusion?

To subdue anxiety/fears/worries/threats?

To promote "regularity"?

To hasten the arrival of buses or trains?

To "get going" on the job?

To stall, procrastinate (to legitimately "goof off")?

As an aid to concentration?

To "ward off" bad news—on the phone, in person?

To get tough (backbone developer) and be able to withstand difficulties?

To appear tough (avoid showing weakness or vulnerability)?

To stay calm under pressure (relieve psychic pressure)?

To appear calm and collected?

To celebrate a point won/a good score/an accomplishment?

To soothe bruised sensitivities if the point is lost/for a poor score/for a missed target?

To cover feelings of inadequacy?

To cover feelings of social awkwardness?

To relieve the emotional discomfort caused by knowing you didn't do an honest job, or make an honest effort, or tell the whole truth?

To subdue rage during and after an argument?

To feel solaced when abused, unrecognized or otherwise sorry for yourself?

To get a physical lift when you're tired?

To relax?

To observe a well-practiced ritual: drinks before dinner?

To observe the TV sacrament: watch, nibble, smoke; watch, nibble, smoke . . . ?

To relieve boredom?

To pay respect to the God of the Night (bedtime ritual)?
To fall asleep again during the night?
To satisfy hunger?
To gratify your mouth's need for attention?
To quell an acidy feeling in your viscera?
To soothe frustration?
Because the pack is there?
Because you think cigarettes taste good?
To celebrate good news?
To complete pleasurable cycles—after sex, a good meal, drinks, good friends and talk, the last run on the ski slope; sitting down to relax after working at a hobby, finishing a project?
To pass time while waiting for someone, or for something to happen (appointments, car pooling, picking up someone after school or the orthodontist, waiting your turn in the doctor's office)?
Because certain sounds trigger a reach for a cigarette (an old song, doorbell, telephone ring, other sounds)?
Because certain odors or fragrances trigger the desire for a cigarette —the smell of a sizzling steak, beer, burning leaves, your lady's distinctive perfume (or your man's), camphor/Lysol/ammonia, chalk dust in a schoolroom, a hard-to-place aroma out of your past . . . ?
Because you're restless?
To keep your hands busy?
To clear your sinuses?
To keep awake while you're driving?
To soothe a headache, cramps, pain?
To start the creative juices flowing, and keep them flowing?
Because everyone is hassling you to quit and you don't like to be pushed around?

Uses overlap and intertwine—but you surely have recognized yourself and certain smoking connections. Most of these are learned conditions; many are easily redirected to less bothersome and less harmful alternatives; many are simply not true physiologically—such as "smoking calms me down." Nicotine is a stimulant; it affects your entire system.

Take comfort in the fact that all these uses are easy to deal with —if you deal with them individually. Together, they're overwhelming and overpowering. That's the fact which discourages most smokers from thinking seriously about stopping. You have to separate them out from one another.

To break cleanly and comfortably from the smoking problem (or almost any "intake" problem—overeating, excess use of caffeine and/or alcohol and perhaps even tranquilizers), you will want to take your habit apart and deal with each element singly.

Consider the motto "United we stand, divided we fall." United, the complex habit you live with is as strong as strands of wires twisted into a cable. Divided, each one is a slender fiber that is easily cut.

Read and follow each section of this book carefully in order to gain control over each element of your habit and deal with it effectively. When you have all the connections disconnected, decide when and how you want to quit smoking, and you'll be ready. At that time you may also want to seek out more direct personal help at a smokEnder seminar.

five

LEARNING HOW TO COPE

How did we get this way—dealing with a hundred tasks, responsibilities and problems, like a juggler in the circus? How can we
take on so much responsibility for others when we can hardly deal
with our own problems?

It's the same for all of us, and it adds up to the same thing.
Tension. Hysteria. Pressure. Short tempers. Guilt. Hostility.
More cigarettes . . . *But do cigarettes really make anything better?*
That's one of the key concepts of the smokEnder program which
all members usually see clearly whether or not they agreed with
it when they entered the program.

In this chapter, I'm going to try to convince you that you can
cope more effectively and less hysterically *without* cigarettes—
and that smoking may, indeed, be one of the causes of your poor
management of some situations. We'll explore some of the reasons why we rely on cigarettes to solve our problems. And we'll
take the new you along to try on both your old and new attitudes
toward the things you deal with every day. Life has an unbelievable way of dealing out sharply agonizing pain and anguish—and,
sometimes simultaneously, magnificent joy and happiness.

Do you ever wonder how some people stand up under misery
and torment? I often think of Mrs. Rose Kennedy and wonder

how she kept her head together through her lifetime of extremes. For most of us, a retarded child is the ultimate in sadness and heartache; Mrs. Kennedy had a retarded child. To lose an eldest son is heartbreaking; Mrs. Kennedy lost her eldest in the war. She lost her daughter Kathleen in a plane crash. Say that the law of compensation balances such sadness, and three of her sons gained prominence in national affairs. One became President, one Attorney General and later a senator, and the third also became a senator. How could she endure to have two sons assassinated? Any one of us must empathize and know we'd have difficulty enduring the agony of lost dreams and promise as well as the pain of losing loved ones. How can Mrs. Kennedy have coped with all this? Her husband had been rendered helpless by a stroke, so that she could not rely upon him for solace. It seems unbearable.

I puzzled about this for years, because I doubt that I could have withstood a quarter of the emotional trauma without coming apart and losing my senses. I read an interview recently in which a journalist asked, "Mrs. Kennedy, we have all wondered how you have been able to cope with the events in your life so courageously." And she responded, "It isn't the events in your life that matter—it's *how you respond* to the events that matters." Mrs. Kennedy learned to cope.

You can cope too. But let's look at some tricks and techniques that can be more helpful than a cigarette.

Sorting It Out

The best way to gain control of your hassles and worries is to put them into tangible form. Then you can deal in a direct, business-like way—instead of feeling that you have a thousand worries, problems, responsibilities. Here's one trick that is borrowed from the best of business management:

Prepare a list of everything that's worrying you—or bugging you. A Bug List. When you've finished your Training to Cope with the help of this book, you should have formed the habit of writing a Bug List for yourself at least once a week, so you can get the accumulation of problems off your chest and get on with taking care of some of the things you can deal with. What really happens is that you put priorities on problems and deal with the most important first. You will also see that some things are really not so serious, some things will repair themselves without any attention (somehow some problems just dry up and blow away if you ignore them) and some of the bugs are just "supposin'" worries.

Earl Nightingale, the famous radio personality, says that 80 percent of the things we worry about never happen, 15 percent we can't do anything about, so we really have only 5 percent to deal with—and that's not too awful.

Let's find the 5 percent. Here's a sample list. Make your own in your notebook and add to it during the week. As you take action on or eliminate an item, draw a line through it. It feels good to have wiped out a worry visibly. And it helps in the future, when you look back and see some of the things you were worried about. It can be almost funny.

But that's a lesson for you, too. You can train yourself not to clutter your head with unnecessary worries and problems.

SAMPLE BUG LIST

RANK (Importance)	ITEM	ACTION NEEDED
#3	Prepare report for Monday	Find 3 hours alone; ask Charlie to discuss best approach; borrow a typewriter.
7	Visit Aunt Tillie in hospital.	Call her to tell her we're thinking of her—will come on Wed. nite.
1	Tuition for State College	Rearrange payment schedule of mortgage? Try for a loan?

RANK (Importance)	ITEM	ACTION NEEDED
5	Mother-in-law lives with us; very little privacy now.	Suggest Sis get a part-time job? Ask boss for a raise? Consider redoing Sis's room as a private studio-type room with a little kitchen for Mother; she needs privacy too.
2	Our anniversary next week! What, when to get a gift and do something about it?	Call the Simmonses, ask them to join us for a day on the slopes to celebrate; or tickets to the concert? Buy a card to send on Tuesday!
4	That cough is getting worse.	Appointment with Dr. Franklin; consider quitting smoking . . .
6	Promised to give a talk at the club next month. Scared; uncomfortable about it.	Decide to do it and get to work learning everything I can about the subject; or decide not to do it and call the chairman today. Get it off my mind.

You have to state a problem before you can solve it. And writing it in this form forces you to put it into a concise statement. Then you can write some meaningful alternatives from which you can choose your best action. Then you can act.

Which brings us to the next condition you should examine in your campaign to restyle your life in order to reduce the need to smoke: anxiety.

ANXIETY

Anxiety is defined as a "painful uneasiness of mind over an impending or anticipated ill." That's Webster. The garden-variety definition is fear and self-doubt over something you can't do anything about, frequently can't even state. (When you know what's bothering you, either do something about it or worry constructively.)

Charlie A., a junior in college, is tense about an economics exam. He's done as much as he can to master the material, but he worries about whether he can get a top grade. For a few days he allows himself a vague sense of coming doom and is helpless to do anything about it. On Sunday night, the night he prepares his Bug List, he has to state the problem. What he discovers is that his problem isn't vague at all: he hadn't given himself enough time to study the material to get his "A." Now he has to develop some alternatives and act on them. The anxiety is reduced, just as a swollen ankle is, in direct proportion to the firmness applied to it. Charlie has two alternatives. He can withdraw temporarily from the student orchestra and free himself for some extra study time; he can spend the weekend at school studying, instead of visiting his girl; he can cut down on his preparation for his other subjects, which is risky, or can resign himself to less than an "A."

Charlie chooses from among the alternatives what he perceives as the best solution. It may be the wrong one, but at least he got off dead center and did something to move his case along and relieve his anxieties.

There are two things to think about. The anxiety alone could cause him to fail in the exam; anxiety seems to paralyze us. Also, life is filled with necessities to make decisions, and the wisest among us realize that we will "win a few, lose a few"—nobody's perfect. How hard are you on yourself? Do you expect always to have the right answer; do the right thing; make the right decision? You need an escape valve.

1. Ask, "Why has this task got to be done?" You may find that you'd been plodding along from habit with a project, using a procedure that is no longer useful.

2. Promise you'll examine your attitudes about tasks you set yourself. Set the goal realistically. Remind yourself that this is an imperfect world.

Once the goal is set, go to it. If you go beyond your goal, that's terrific, but not necessary.

3. "Is there a better way to do it?" Often we inherit obsolete practices and never stop to reexamine the procedure.

4. Do the very best you can.

President Carter, in his first "chat" with the American people shortly after his inauguration, pledged to "Do the best I can"; and, he added, "I'll make some mistakes . . ." To be comfortable with yourself, you must be honest with yourself. Do the best you can.

When we start making excuses for our behavior, we get into emotional trouble and smoke more. How often do you hear someone say, "Well, I didn't know you wanted that today." That's one example of the kind of "excuse" that puts us down in our own eyes.

To sum up, here's how to deal with anxiety and frustration and reduce your need to smoke:

1. Ask: Why is this really necessary? If you find it isn't, give it a low priority on your Bug List.
2. Ask: What is to be accomplished? Set a realistic goal. State what should happen, by when, to what degree (or in what amount), at what cost in time and money.
3. Ask: Is there a better way to do it? Faster, shorter, pleasanter, cleaner, cheaper . . .
4. Do it! And do the best you can.

STRESS

Many smokers feel that they can't quit because their lives are so stressful and that smoking puts them on an "even keel." It's not surprising that we feel that way. We've been told that smoking steadies our nerves.

I used that excuse too, and whenever I did without my cigarettes for a couple of hours or days, I became an animal. So, I reasoned, cigarettes keep me calm.

But it isn't quite like that. I was unprepared to "do without" my dose of nicotine and my "old buddy." I felt physically rotten and emotionally deprived. I was angry with myself and everyone in the world for having had this dirty trick played on me.

I'm delighted to assure you it doesn't have to be like that. You can prepare yourself emotionally and physically for the time when you choose to quit—and you can do it with a smile on your face.

Our Bodies

How can a stimulant act to calm us down? I'd like to describe another scene in the average smoker's routine. When Jeremy wakes up, he reaches for a cigarette to get himself going. What gets him going? Nicotine.

Smoking a cigarette introduces nicotine into the system via the soft tissues of the mouth as well as through the lungs. The body reacts violently, since nicotine is a poison. The reaction causes a flow of adrenaline and other hormones which bring us to a higher alertness and gives us (briefly) increased energy in a crisis by elevating our blood-sugar level. This causes a momentary "lift"; it is followed, however, by a too-rapid movement of glucose out of the blood after the "danger" is past, and the result is a feeling of fatigue. Fatigue causes anxiety, self-pity, low-grade dissatisfaction and general discomfort—which, for a smoker, is a signal to reach for the pickup in a cigarette.

Consider the fact that you repeat this process twenty, thirty or forty times a day and for however many years you have smoked. (I repeated it about forty times a day for twenty-two years.)

If you could see inside your body—as in the old Alka-Selzer ads —you'd see a lot of action. In addition to glands' squirting adrenaline, your pancreas is busily dealing with the glycogen your liver is shooting. All this produces a temporary rise in your blood pressure, which increases your heartbeat rate by at least 9 beats per minute (around 10,000 extra beats per day), and all that activity apparently influences the levels of fats circulating in the bloodstream.

At the same time, the red blood cells are obstructed from their mission of carrying oxygen to the heart and brain because of the carbon monoxide and other gases in the cigarette smoke. In fact, "as much as 20% of the blood pushed around by the heart of the smoker is not working so far as carrying oxygen is concerned. Since the heart has the highest oxygen requirement per unit weight of any tissue, any change in the supply of oxygen could affect the heart first, and thereby increase the risk of an attack for the smoker."*

This marvelous machine, the body, has an additional mechanism working to stabilize these ups and downs—another law of nature at work: "to every action there is an equal and opposite reaction." Indeed, after this swift high, the body, in its attempt to maintain itself at a constant level, drops into a depressed state —below the level of comfort—as it replenishes the supply of hormones, enzymes and sugars that have just been expended in combat. You feel blah. It's not imaginary.

So Jerry reaches for something to give him another lift. This time he reaches for coffee.

Coffee is also a stimulant, as you know: it constricts the blood vessels and starts the heart pounding and the blood pressure zooming. The lift can be so potent, you shake. Coffee nerves aren't imaginary. On the way to work Jerry has two more cigarettes, and around ten o'clock begins to think about a break for coffee. As we know, blood sugar should be maintained at a certain level of comfort. If one has too much, he has diabetes; if too little, hypoglycemia. Most of us have a properly functioning system, but when we burn up more sugar than we have in reserve because of increased emotional or physical demand we feel weak, or woozy, or light-headed. Dr. Alton Ochsner, in his book *Smoking and*

---

*William Likoff, M.D.; Bernard Segal, M.D., and Lawrence Galton, *Your Heart* (Philadelphia: Lippincott, 1972), p. 175.

Health, refers to this condition as the "Blind Staggers." If you have it, you know what he means. He finds that smoking causes the level of blood sugar to drop. When your blood-sugar level is low, you certainly look for a lift—but a cigarette isn't able to boost you up high enough, so you go for coffee, and the combination of the caffeine and the nicotine does the job. So Jerry can work until lunchtime. Lunch is something like a hamburger, French fries and coffee or Coke—and a couple of cigarettes. About three o'clock, Jerry becomes weak and twitchy again. So he has another coffee or a Coke, or iced tea—it's the same shot of caffeine—with a couple of cigarettes.

By now Jerry is so hyped up he can't sustain his energy level very long, and he may start chewing on candy or, if it's available, drink some beer or other alcohol. His body is begging for sugar and he responds to it.

He gets home really tired; has dinner after a drink or two; smokes; has some more coffee very likely; smokes; watches TV or goes out for the evening; smokes; drinks coffee, beer or liquor; comes home; has a snack and some more coffee and a final cigarette.

In the morning he wonders why he feels tired. It's because he's drugged and worn out. His body has never had a chance to build up reserve resources; he constantly overdraws his account in his energy bank. It's not hard to understand why smokers' hearts give way sooner than those of nonsmokers.

"Well," you say, "what should Jerry do instead of running in that rat race he's caught in? In fact, what should *I* do?" Because, very likely you're caught in it too. Here are the secrets of coping with fatigue, tension, stress:

The best way to treat fatigue is to prevent it from occurring. Fatigue can be caused by insufficient rest, insufficient food, improper foods, excess smoking/caffeine/alcohol. Plan to get sufficient rest. When your body is in the best possible condition, the big event of quitting becomes easier.

Change your eating habits to avoid fatigue. Carbohydrates

(sugars) cause a rapid response by the body—a quick rise and an equally quick fall of blood sugar. Protein slows the process down considerably. Knowing that simple fact, you can arrange to eat sufficient protein at every meal to counterbalance whatever carbohydrate you take in. My own mental scale allows about two or three times as much protein as carbo. One egg balances a half slice of bread; a hamburger balances one slice of bread or half of a bun; a steak balances a small piece of pie. Use your best judgment from your own experience, but work on this if you want to gain energy even if you choose to continue to smoke for some additional time. Here's what I learned. The "hunger" I would feel during the day and the weakness that came upon me at various times seem to have occurred on days when I had high-carbo meals. When we'd go skiing in Vermont, I'd have a typical New England breakfast of pancakes and syrup, all I could eat. By the time we got to the slopes, I'd be "hungry" and weak. And cranky!

After I learned to increase my protein and reduce my carbo, I had lots of pep—and as a plus, I could eat far less without feeling hungry. I rarely go "limp" a couple of hours after breakfast or lunch unless I have a typical fast-food lunch. Or unless my day brings a huge emotional crisis, which burns up more sugar than I'm prepared for. To get a boost I've learned to carry protein tablets, or I drink a small glass of orange juice. Orange juice contains a specific sugar which is quickly and easily absorbed into the system. The vitamin C in orange juice also helps when you smoke: nicotine robs the system of vitamin C, so while you smoke, you need all the extra vitamin C you can get.

But how is all this applied to your ability to quit smoking? Simply this: if you prevent that weak and weary feeling which is caused by a drop in your blood sugar, you will have eliminated one very important need for cigarettes. *The less often you reach for a cigarette to give yourself a lift, the less need you'll have for a lift.*

Here is a summary of action you can take to avoid fatigue, self-pity and stress:

1. Be good to yourself. Treat yourself with the greatest possible

respect—as you would an honored friend. Be willing to rearrange your priorities as you would for your best friend. Put yourself and your personal needs first for the next ten days. (Within that time, you should be able to sort out certain frustrations and plan to deal with them; repattern some counterproductive and worn-out routines; bring yourself up to the best possible physical and emotional state; view your smoking behavior honestly and be in a position to decide whether you choose to quit smoking—or continue for a while.)

2. Command yourself to get sufficient rest. It's much easier to think and act when you're not tired; life becomes less pressured —which means you have less need to smoke. It's easier to quit smoking when your body is in the best condition. Just as an athlete prepares for the big event, you must too.

3. Consider eating six small meals a day instead of two or three larger ones. This is a fine weight-control device, as well as a means of eliminating fatigue. For instance, breakfast at 8, mini-meal at 11, lunch around 2, mini-meal around 4, dinner at 7, mini-meal around 10 at night. You eat before you get hungry, and you won't eat more than your body can handle. You won't be logy and sleepy after such meals. Each regular meal will become smaller because the mini-meals will have reduced your appetite. The mini-meals should consist of a fruit or vegetable and some protein. A glass of milk (nonfat) and a banana is a fine mini-meal, or a chunk of meat and an apple is good. Even if you work, these little meals can be packed without too much trouble. If you're determined to do it, you'll find a way.

4. Arrange to have a high protein intake at each meal. This means you should start the day with a real breakfast. If you haven't been taking the time—or if you've been telling yourself you don't eat breakfast as a weight-control measure—you will be surprised at how much good this will do you. At lunch, avoid the sandwich or hamburger trap. Offset bread with meat for the correct balance of protein to starch. Or order something that is eaten without bread around it. Observe your eating habits; de-

velop your own balance. Think of it as a challenging puzzle.

5. When you feel physically low, "touchy" or irritable, or generally weary and fatigued, reach for a small glass of orange juice (unless, of course, you have a medical condition, such as diabetes, that prohibits orange juice). Milk is wonderful for a pickup, too, but for different reasons. Maybe not as fast-acting, but much more lasting.

(Incidentally, I've found milk is a terrific friend even after you quit smoking; it does wonders for the nerves.)

6. Have a glass of milk before going to bed. It not only improves the quality of your rest, but gives your body, during the night, a reserve of proper nourishment, which is transformed into pep and energy for when you wake up. If you wake up refreshed, that's one less cigarette you need.

7. Learn to relax, quickly and deeply. We have a Relaxation Ritual in the smokEnder program which we teach by demonstration and practice, but you can create a combination of the necessary elements for yourself in a routine that suits your own personal taste. Here are the elements:

Assume a "hang loose" posture. Go limp.

Visualize a soothing, pleasing situation.

Get away from it all for a moment.

Concentrate on that image and nothing else. If it's a sailboat, for instance, stare at it in your mind's eye. Don't waver. Now put it all together by taking a very slow and deep breath. Come up for air, as necessary, and repeat two or three times.

You will feel relaxed and refreshed—and will have eliminated the need for a few more cigarettes.

Add a "sales pitch" to yourself: start with "I really want to quit smoking." After you have stopped smoking, you can change the script to "I really want to learn French," or lose weight, or find a better job, or whatever.

This really works. If you wonder about it, consider the effectiveness of the ads on consumer sales in this country. How many products are you buying and using now that you didn't know existed not long ago? Why are you using them? Do you really need them? You were "programmed" to want them. You were convinced they were essential to your well-being or image or whatever. That's how advertising works.

Now, "program" yourself to want to quit smoking. I assure you you can, if you care enough about yourself to take the time and make the simple effort necessary to know yourself, accept yourself and grow up that last little bit.

In addition to the above suggestion, or instead of it, you may want to use meditation as a means of relaxing. You might want to look into the TM program—which appears to be doing an effective job for many people; or you might benefit from reading *The Relaxation Response* by Herbert Benson, M.D. (Avon). They both deal with the same mechanism, but I find the accountability and in-person approach provided by a program most helpful.

8. Get your circulation going. You know, of course, the benefit of a healthy body maintained by good circulation. It's the circulating blood that freshens all your organs, nourishes, cleans, oxygenates and generally tidies up—carrying off dead material and poisons like a good housekeeper. Too often we're so sedentary that our circulation slows down, I suspect, to the speed of cold molasses. With a little encouragement, your circulation can pick up its pace and give you bonus benefits you may not have thought about. For instance, in addition to carrying off nicotine faster, improved circulation will put color in your cheeks (that's why a lot of smokers have a pasty pallor—smoking restricts the circulation to the surface of your skin); your bowel functions will become more regular; you'll start feeling better.

How do you get your circulation going? Any of the usual tricks, sports, machines. The secret is to find something you enjoy doing and make it routine. Promise yourself, at first, to do just five minutes three mornings a week. And then, as William James, the father of modern psychology, said about habit formation, "never suffer an exception" to your practice of a new habit until it is ingrained.

There are some fine books on the subject, any of them worthwhile if you follow it. I like *Total Fitness in 30 Minutes a Week* by Laurence E. Morehouse, Ph.D., and Leonard Gross (Simon and Schuster) for its practical, concise approach. In addition, I follow a very satisfying exercise routine designed by my daughter Lilla for herself. (See her sketch at the back of the book.) She's a slim, agile young artist/dancer, with endless energy now. And since I quit smoking and started these exercises, I too seem to have an abundance of energy.

I also recommend Richard Hittleman's *Yoga 28 Day Exercise Plan* (Bantam).

9. Learn to love water. To wake yourself up in the morning, have some water! I prefer it cold—a big glass of cold, clear water. Some people like to drink a cup of hot water with lemon first thing in the morning. That too really wakes you up—and gets your circulation going as well as your digestive system. And it eliminates the need for a cigarette as soon as you awaken.

Water beats all the soft-drink promises to refresh. Try it inside and out: wash your hands and face with cool water, and then have a good glass of cold water. Water isn't generally a "cue" for a cigarette the way a Coke or coffee is—you can probably eliminate another couple of cigarettes.

Water is a powerful weight controller. If you drink a glass of water before you eat, you won't eat as much. Your stomach will feel fuller sooner. Many people drink a glass of water before retiring as an aid to regularity. (That's great if you haven't a bladder problem that awakens you at night.)

And in addition to all the other benefits, I believe the water somehow helps flush out the poisons—including the nicotine. Altogether a wonderful and inexpensive "treatment."

10. Pamper yourself! Do nice things for yourself. Get into the habit of rewarding yourself with special treats. Take time off to read; take a walk, a bubble bath; visit or call a friend; spend some time on a favorite hobby; shop for something you'd like (within your budget; soon, after you stop smoking, you'll have hundreds

of dollars a year to spend on frivolous treats instead of on cigarettes). The smokEnder "Cost of Smoking" Chart at the back of the book shows how much you'll "earn" by not smoking.

11. Pay attention to your appearance. Look as handsome or as lovely as possible. Change the style or color of your hair; add some excitement to your wardrobe. If you "look sharp" the chances are you'll "feel sharp," with apologies to the razor-blade company that made that expression famous.

12. Sort the junk out of your life. Be occupied with activities that are truly meaningful, satisfying and important to you. You surely have more things to do than you have time for. Eliminate the trivia unless they're fun. For now, don't become involved in anything unless it has some meaning for you. Chase martyrdom out of your life. You don't have to prove anything to anyone anymore. You're no longer a child. By this time in your life, you have been very successful in many things. Review the first chapter to recall those things you're proud of. Treat yourself with respect, and then "treat" yourself and reward yourself. As the ads said, "For a treat instead of a treatment."

13. Add some spontaneity and excitement to your life. Bob Conklin, in his book *Dynamics of Success* (Prentice-Hall), says that "Without 'expectation' you are mentally dead." He goes on to show how people who have no expectations accomplish very little and are dull. "Life is dull to people who are dull" is a common expression. And boredom is a big cause of smoking.

There are ways to alleviate loneliness and boredom. Making yourself important to other people is an obvious one. Find those who need your talents, experience, caring, time or money, if you have any extra, and help. You'll need good judgment to prevent yourself from becoming a busybody, an intruder or a dictatorial rich uncle. Take an interest in other people, sports, hobbies etc.

14. Deal with your guilt. Even when you're very busy, very much occupied with your work, with your family, friends, community, something can still seem to be missing. Consider for a moment the possibility that your smoking has placed a "smoke

screen" between you and the joy and beauty of life. For some of us, the very fact that we know smoking is a form of self-destruction causes us to put life down. Guilt plays a strong hand. "Life can't be so great," we almost say, "or I'd cherish it and not risk it by smoking." Many smokers develop a blind spot to looking ahead over the years.

Now, this gets rather complicated, as I have learned from my own experience and from hundreds of smokers who have talked with me. Because we feel guilty about our smoking and "self-destruction," we lose some respect for ourselves each time we light up. I recall the case of a judge who went through the smokEnder program some time ago. He was a very distinguished man; very much in control of his life, as you might imagine—except for his smoking. He said to me, "Jackie, you know I have attained a modicum of achievement in my field and I am respected for my accomplishment. People look up to me. But *I* don't!" He thought little of himself because he couldn't control his own smoking; he considered himself a fraud. After he quit smoking, he regained his self-respect and experienced a tremendous sense of liberation.

Guilt frequently spirals down to another human response that isn't too pretty. People often resort to martyr tactics in order to obtain reassurance that they are okay. They'll put themselves out for anyone, anytime. What they're really saying is "I'm not so bad, am I? Look what I'm doing for you. Surely that proves that I have a lot of good in me." There are an infinite number of variations to this script. And people let you throw yourself under their feet as a doormat. They don't respect you for it—but you put yourself in the position of being available to be used. Why are you the one who drives the car pool so that everyone else can go to the big game? Why are you the last one in the office each night from your department? Why are you the one who scrapes the mud, carries the whole load, brings up the rear, stays outside to wait for the delivery while everyone else is inside having a good time? Why? Because you want to be a martyr and hope that someone will say, "What a dear person you are—so *good!*"

And because nobody says that, and nobody treats you with the respect you crave, you begin to feel sorry for yourself. Poor me! We're back to that again. So you light up to soothe your poor ego.

Let's do something about that!

A New Assurance

Let's yank the "smoke screen" away from your eyes. Reassure yourself that life is terrific, worth living. Take stock of what you're looking forward to. Make a list right now, and keep adding to it. Permit yourself a ray of hope that you will stop smoking soon and that when you do, the impetus of pride and confidence in your accomplishment will propel you to better things.

To get your engine warmed up, to help you overcome the inertia of breaking through that smoke screen which made life too often seem dull and lifeless, here's a good lead.

Create expectations and surprises. That's a form of reward, too, but it takes a little help to get your creativity going to make it happen.

Bob Conklin asks us to use Mind Motivators to stir creativity. These Mind Motivators are simple questions, similar to those children ask. He asks us to open our eyes with expectation and wonder. Asking "why" and "what" begins a chain reaction of "I wish," and then "I will."

In the smokEnder program we suggest to our smoker members that they plan new and interesting things they've never done before or haven't had time to do in a long time.

"What would I really like to do next time I have a half hour or a day free? What did I use to like to do that I haven't done in months? Years? Where can I go that will be refreshingly different?"

Keep a list of good ideas in your book so that you will remember them when you have some time. I still do that and am surprised at the number of fine ideas I've collected during the years.

Children have to see and touch and experience. Curiosity and the expectation of excitement are as much a part of childhood as growing. Somewhere through the years we buried all that. Why? To be sophisticated? Or because we're too busy?

Dig it out again! Fill your life with expectations and childlike adventures. When you stop smoking, you will have lovely habits with which to reward yourself. The nicer you are to yourself the less you need to reward yourself with a cigarette.

Now let's get back to the business of being a martyr.

For the smoker who quits smoking successfully by following the smokEnder concept of regaining self-respect and understanding the ego involvement of the smoking habit, a return of, or increase in, self-esteem is certain.

An early and visible sign of this is a self-assertiveness or independence on the part of the ex-smoker. The following observation was written by a 1969 smokEnder graduate, who later became a sensitive Moderator (teacher in the program) and successfully aided hundreds of smokers who attended her seminars in Pennsylvania. As of this writing, Lois Rafalko is still teaching people to free themselves from the habit and has advanced in the organization to become Program Coordinator in the Phillipsburg, New Jersey, headquarters where all the mail from smokers and smokEnder graduates descends. She and I have read thousands of comments from smokers and ex-smokers; her observations are based upon her own experiences as a smoker—as a Moderator—and as a person exposed to vast amounts of smoking behavior.

"He [the ex-smoker] becomes unwilling to be imposed upon, intolerant of being taken for granted and will not, in any sense, be a martyr. This new assertiveness (usually noticed first by his immediate family) often represents an abrupt change in his behavior and may be misinterpreted by others (especially smokers) as irritability—due to kicking the habit.

"The smokEnder may begin speaking out in situations where he previously remained quiet, though he may have seethed inside.

For example, he may stand up to a wife (or husband or child) who has usually gotten her way . . . he may begin to complain about poor service or shoddy merchandise for which he is paying . . . he may even create a small scene in a supermarket over a man with a loaded grocery cart who is holding up an 'express' checkout line. He is asserting his own rights more firmly than before—because he has a new or stronger self-esteem.

"When this new attitude first rubs against people who are accustomed to the old behavior—it causes friction and other people tend to react by thinking, 'What's wrong with Joe?'

"One normally very shy and quiet smokEnder, buoyed by her new victory over her smoking habit, found the courage to tell off a bully in the presence of a number of other people at a club meeting. When she got home from the meeting, she received several phone calls from friends, asking, 'What's wrong with you?' or 'Are you all right?'

"Members frequently hear remarks such as 'you're really irritable since you quit smoking' or 'why don't you have a cigarette to calm your nerves?'

"The danger here lies in the fact that if this situation is repeated often enough, the smokEnder, himself, may begin to believe he is 'irritable' because he is not smoking. Sometimes members return to meetings after they stop smoking and say, 'I've been very irritable this week . . . my husband (or wife or child) tells me I've been very touchy (or edgy or snappish) since I quit smoking.'

"Smokers should be warned of this possibility; we should explain the difference between his real motivation—self-respect—a positive trait, and nervous irritation, a negative one (which is common to those smokers who quit without proper motivation).

"If the member knows what is happening to him and why, no matter how often his mood is misinterpreted he will be able to see his behavior as a positive response and be reinforced by it."

So, surely, there's another big step in your self-knowledge. You must allow yourself to assert yourself—instead of smoking; and you must anticipate the jibes of friends and relatives in response to your newfound self-respect.

We discuss assertiveness and aggressiveness frequently in the program and clarify the difference between the two. So often people have picked up the habit of defensiveness and aggressiveness and wonder why life seems so tough. These are the people who have come to believe they must be direct and honest in their dealings with others—to a fault. Tact and diplomacy are out of their frame of reference. "I'll tell somebody they stink, if they do," I've heard a woman say. "Why would you tell them that?" I asked. "Well," she said, "because I believe in saying exactly what I think so people know where they stand with me."

This same woman, a prototype of many other men and women I've dealt with in the smokEnder program, later indicated that one of her problems is that she feels people are often against her. She was unable to develop the number of both casual and close friends she would have liked, and she couldn't understand why. Also, typical of the pattern, she bristled when anyone criticized her, first denying the criticism and then assaulting the critic.

The final stage of the pattern is repentance. She regretted immediately saying the things she had said and the tone of voice she had used, and very often she tried to repair the damage by being supersweet. I would say she was a passionate smoker—so many situations caused her to light up involuntarily. As I recall, this particular person smoked about two and a half packs a day for thirty years.

The happy ending is that she stopped smoking very comfortably—after she understood how immature her behavior was—and she stopped being defensive and became assertive rather than aggressive.

Courses in assertiveness training are popular in many cities, and there are many books worth reading on the subject. The book *When I Say No I Feel Guilty* by Manuel J. Smith, Ph.D. (Bantam) clearly describes situations and scripts for responses to get one into the swing.

Before you can quit smoking comfortably, you will want to reduce a number of unnecessary stressful situations caused by difficulties with interpersonal relationships.

REWARD/GUILT/MARTYRDOM

It is important that we understand how the reward concept relates to the human "need" to smoke, in order to expose self-pity, martyrdom and guilt.

The human "need" to smoke grows out of an addiction to nicotine and becomes a compulsion. The addictive need is then augmented by a second "need": to react repeatedly according to conditioned responses that have developed concurrently. The third need that emerges is the need for an escape valve, for self-expression, for recognition and ultimately for reward. It is this third area which requires further examination.

Eric Berne, M.D., in his book *Games People Play* presents one explanation for this "recognition-reward" need. He suggests that infantile stimulus-hunger emerges into a pattern of behavior that he calls "recognition-hunger." This can be satisfied by "stroking" —a term generally used to mean intimate physical contact (such as the stroking or patting of a baby). Dr. Berne extends this term to mean any act that implies recognition of another's presence. A "stroke" may be thought of as the fundamental unit of social action. (Smokers may well be using each cigarette as a "stroke," a counterfeit means of satisfying the need induced by recognition-hunger—or, in other words, of satisfying one's ego.)

We all need some form of stroking—praise, a pat on the back, appreciation: a reward to confirm how good we are, to confirm that we exist. This recognition for which we hunger comes all too rarely. Our boss, our mate, our children and our colleagues usually complain to us much more than they thank us or express appreciation. As a result, we may have narcissistically conferred the property of "reward" upon our cigarette (as the ads tell us)—the pat on the back that says, "You've done a really good job." It isn't much, but a smoker is willing to settle for it.

"Smoking" does not recognize your goodness. In fact, it really makes most smokers feel guilty because they know it is self-destructive. When we have this guilt, we feel we deserve punishment; guilt erodes self-respect. In keeping, perhaps, with the Puritan Ethic, we offer ourselves up to be punished and at the same time to gain the approval that will shore up our self-respect. The smoker becomes a willing martyr.

The smoker must learn to reward himself in a less self-defeating way, but he cannot achieve this until he feels good about himself. Motivations and needs are always changing. The smoker's needs change as he goes through the program. He must be taught to handle these changing needs and encouraged to quit smoking *for himself* because he likes himself. Therefore, the Moderator leads the smoker through the following paces:

1. You're no longer a child, so stop seeking external recognition.
2. You will think better of yourself and throw off guilt when you quit smoking.
3. As self-image improves, self-pity is eliminated and self-respect returns.
4. Self-satisfaction becomes the ultimate reward, since you are doing something for yourself because you like yourself.

The smoker learns he doesn't need external recognition anymore. When he has done a good job, he can feel proud. That is internal recognition. It is having grown up. And when he needs confirmation of his existence, his polished, shiny, clean new ego will give him that reassurance. It is then that he will really be his own person. He can truly be free and not need to smoke!

Don't Smoke—Stroke! There's nothing like a strong dose of honest self-mastery to enhance one's image to oneself. This spirals upward into a form of self-respect which can't be bought.And the upward success spiral "infects" other areas of your life so that you welcome new challenges. You become a winner.

six

RATIONALIZATIONS

If I were still polishing my rationalizations and trying to evade the pressures to quit smoking, I'd find comfort in the new thrust of the government—and the eager cooperation of the cigarette companies—to produce a low-tar cigarette. The smoker in me would quickly categorize this as the safe cigarette. Happy day! I'd say; I always knew they'd find a way to beat the health and disease threat. And I'd close my eyes and ears for a few more years.

This is what we in smokEnders call the Low Tar Rip-Off. Here's how it works: The government, the American Cancer Society and others who are concerned that smokers are not heeding their advice decided that the most productive effort would be to provide them with a less hazardous means of indulging their habit. For a few years they campaigned to persuade smokers to consider some tricks for reducing the danger: don't inhale; don't smoke more than two-thirds of the cigarette; switch to a low-tar cigarette. (If it hadn't cost so much money, I would have been amused at the naiveté. A smoker who continues to smoke in the face of the evidence isn't likely to have much success in not inhaling. Or in remembering to smoke only part of the cigarette.)

The results were rather disappointing to lawmakers and health educators. The next step was a gigantic movement toward developing a more innocuous cigarette. Ironically, the government took over the responsibility, and the cost. That puzzles me. I should have thought the cost of new-product research and development might have fallen to the corporations which stand to benefit from the results, as with drugs or any other consumer product. The windfall to the tobacco industry is shown, now, in its supergracious cooperation with the health people to provide us with many "less hazardous" cigarettes.

What makes me sad is that we're being ripped off. The fact is that there can never be a safe material or combination of materials for us to inhale into our lungs in the combustible (smoky) state. It doesn't matter if it's fig leaves or orange rinds—if it's burning and produces smoke, and you inhale it, you're causing yourself problems. But the larger cause for sadness is that many smokers will continue to smoke in the false belief that they're safe—and by the time they realize that they're not safe, it could be too late. It's one hell of a form of prevention; I hope you don't fall for it.

Actually, there is greater danger in smoking low–tar/nicotine cigarettes than in smoking regular cigarettes—and that's bad enough. Here are a few reasons: Nicotine is addictive. Therefore, if you switch to low–tar/nicotine brands, you will compensate by smoking more cigarettes; by inhaling more deeply; by puffing more frequently—all to maintain the "comfort" level of nicotine in your bloodstream.

There seems to be far greater production of deadly gases, like carbon monoxide, given off by low–tar/nicotine brands. And because you feel "safe," you throw caution to the wind and smoke without limit.

In its February 21, 1977, Behavior section, *Time* ran an article that quoted Columbia University psychologist Stanley Schachter's opinion about the smoking problem in a report of his findings from a four-year experiment to determine, among other things, the relationship of smoking to stress. "We smoke because we're physically addicted to nicotine. Period. Smoking doesn't reduce anxiety or calm the nerves." Nonsmokers endured the same degrees of stress and pressure in tests.

"Current low tar/nicotine brands may be lethal. You wind up spending more, smoking more and getting far more dangerous combustion products for the same nicotine payoff as stronger cigarettes."

In an aside, Dr. Schacter observed a more serious problem as a result of the low–tar/nicotine brands. He feels it's very likely that the low-tar brands are hooking millions of teen-agers. "When I was young [he was born in 1922], that first Camel or Lucky made so many kids sick that they stayed off cigarettes for good. Now so many brands are so weak that the kids don't get sick enough to stop right away. They just get hooked."

So that you may respect him not only as a scientist but also as a man who understands the problem, it is significant to know that Dr. Schachter is a chain smoker.

I suspect you've discovered that your feelings and reactions to smoking are much like other smokers'. That may be a comfort to you. Your difficulties aren't unique.

One thing we share is our ability to rationalize. Oddly, we all seem to create the same rationalizations. I thought I had invented some of the expressions I used when I was defending my smoking habit until I began hearing strangers use exactly the same words. And I have since heard the same rationalizations thousands of times from the thousands of smokers with whom I come in contact.

Here are most of the rationalizations I've caught in the net. Laugh at them or feel free to borrow some new ones until you're ready to quit.

First I'd like to tell you why I believe we create these "cover stories." I used to wonder about why I said weird things like "Well, I've got to die of something; I might as well die happy" when someone asked me if I realized I was killing myself. But really, what was I supposed to tell them? "Yes, I know, Mr. Jones, but I'm really a yellow-livered, weak-willed dummy with a death wish"? My ego couldn't take that kind of admission (although that was about the extent of my feeling about myself in regard to my smoking). It was hard for me to admit I was out of control. I remember one man, a stranger, who watched me fussing with a baby carriage I was adjusting while smoking, of course. He came over and said, "I wonder if you realize how awful you look tending that little baby with a cigarette hanging out of your mouth." And he crossed the street before I could even acknowledge that he had spoken to me. I resented anyone's interference; smoking was my own business; I'd be my own conscience, thank you. Deep down, however, I knew the others were right. Therefore, I invented some more rationalizations.

I remember my prize one. It went like this:

"There's a direct correlation between my smoking and my ability to perform, produce or create. The less I smoke, the less I can do." This seemed to be particularly true when I worked in my art studio. If I didn't smoke, I seemed to just stand around paralyzed. I now know how difficult it was for me to overcome the variety of triggers inherent in that activity. Linseed oil and turpentine were two strong odor triggers; the conditioned-response aspect was well entrenched, since I can't remember painting and not smoking. (I'm happy to report that I very easily broke all the conditions once I was aware of them. I now have no trouble painting without smoking—except that I have very little time for it now!)

I thought that was an ingenious rationalization. I've since heard it hundreds of times—from all the artists and writers who had smoked and quit.

Another, probably the most used, is "But I enjoy smoking." You may have said it yourself from time to time. What you will learn about the relief from self-induced discomfort should help illuminate the "enjoyment" misconception. How many of the cigarettes you smoke do you enjoy? If you smoked only one or two, we could all relax. But unfortunately, if you're an average smoker, you consume about thirty cigarettes a day. That's a lot of tar, nicotine and gases for small "enjoyment."

I sometimes compare the desire to enjoy a few cigarettes with my love of pecan pie. I could enjoy a piece of pecan pie every day —maybe even two pieces a day. But I'll tell you this: I wouldn't walk a mile for it—nor would I throw a temper tantrum and get downright nasty if I couldn't have a piece when I wanted it. It's one thing to enjoy something on an I-can-take-it-or-leave-it basis. It's another to be compulsive about it.

I suggest you observe your own smoking for the next couple of days and try to establish how many cigarettes you consider enjoyable. If you feel you enjoy more than two a day, I predict you're not quite ready to quit smoking. You must be reading this because someone is pushing you to quit.

The next-most-used old saw is "I can quit anytime I want to!" Generally, this is from youngsters who are just starting to smoke, or from old-time smokers who usually say it as they cough their heads off. It's too bad that kids think they won't get hooked, but I can understand why. They really have never been told that nicotine is an addicting agent and that addiction to it is as demanding as any other addiction. They should be told that many alcoholics and drug addicts confess they had a harder time trying to quit smoking than quitting alcohol or drugs. We'll discuss the addictive aspect of smoking in a later chapter.

Before you become discouraged by what I say about smoking's being tougher to kick than alcohol or drugs, let me say that the process is not tough if it's spelled out for you and you're given the proper guidance. And the physical withdrawal is not as horrible as with the heavy drugs and alcohol. Nicotine is out of your system in three days.

Back to the cougher who insists he can quit anytime he wants to: when he's asked why he doesn't quit, then, since he seems to have a bad cough, the response is standard: "My cough has nothing to do with cigarettes. It's a cold I've been trying to get rid of." I sympathize. How awful to expect him to admit he can't quit. The cough probably increases his anxiety about his health, and anxiety, as you know, causes increased smoking.

Here's another popular number: "It's my only vice—the only thing I really do just for me." The implication is that "I do so much for everyone—my family, my job, my community, everyone —I really don't get any payoff except this simple little indulgence." What you can hear if you listen carefully is "poor me." Often this is followed by "I don't spend a lot of money on drink or clothes for myself or any other extravagances." (I used this one a lot.)

And another one, as well. I was pleased that the raging controversy was about *whether or not* smoking caused cancer. I would argue with Jon, my husband, that he exaggerated the seriousness of the problem. And I would not consider the fact that smoking might cause many other problems for my body. Cancer was the big thing, so I'd say, "I don't believe all that scare stuff. Anyhow, nothing has been *proved*—I've heard and read that many times, even in the medical journals!" There are still articles like that around, and we smokers are sharp-eyed at finding them, just as we're good at sudden blindness when articles appear that offer hard evidence of diseases and damage caused by smoking.

I remember a handsome young pediatrician who went through the smokEnder program in Hunterdon County, New Jersey, some years ago. At his graduation, he asked to say a few words about the peculiar grip smoking can have on otherwise rational people. He described his habit in reading the medical journals: if he spotted anything to do with smoking, he quickly tucked the publication on the bottom of his reading pile. He confessed he had not read one single article about smoking for six years. Up until the time his wife had joined smokEnders several months before him, he had felt trapped. He had tried to quit many times by himself on impulse and had finally surrendered to the belief that he would probably never quit smoking. And it was too uncomfortable for him to read the facts. So he hid behind the statement that "nothing has been clinically proved yet to indicate that smoking really causes cancer."

The key word here is "clinically." It can't be proved in the way other medical tests are conducted. It is outrageous to expect that scientists would induce cancer in live human beings. So no clinical tests on humans have been done. Therefore "nothing has been *clinically* proved."

But wait a minute. There are some interesting clinical experiments coming along. One famous one, done with dogs that were hooked up to smoking machines and "taught" to smoke regularly, produced two significant results. First, when the dogs were unhooked from the machine, they "climbed the walls" and howled for their smoke—which proves the addictive qualities of tobacco. Second, the tests demonstrated that precancerous tissue was found in the dogs' respiratory tracts. In those dogs which were unhooked from the smoking machines the possibility of cancer was apparently reversed and the precancerous tissue reverted to normal. A significant number of the dogs that were kept on the smoking machines succumbed to cancer. The experiment was conducted by one of the most renowned and respected scientists in the field, Dr. Oscar Auerbach, who was working at the Veterans Administration hospital in East Orange, New Jersey.

Although this sort of evidence would convince me, it wouldn't get me to stop smoking—only to stop using that rationalization, maybe.

But let me digress to make the point right here about damage caused by smoking. We actually see thousands of smokers in our seminars. Many come in pale and gasping, fighting for their breath. When they graduate, having been free from smoking for four weeks, these people are breathing easily and the color has returned to their cheeks. I receive hundreds of letters from people who say their new ability to walk around the block is a miracle. It's no miracle. The lungs can't handle the overload of tar, gases and particulate matter and a bronchial impairment. When they stopped smoking, their bodies became much more efficient. It's incredible the amount of coughing we hear at our first session compared with the last. The first session sounds like a polyphonal chorus; there's hardly a moment when someone isn't coughing or clearing his throat. At the last meeting, there's only an occasional cough. Even forty-five- and fifty-year smokers with coughs that seem to tear them apart discover to their amazement that the cough disappears within the first week of not smoking.

I remember a man who came to one of the first meetings in Bethlehem, Pennsylvania. He told us he was 79 years old and smoked about 40 cigarettes a day, some of which he rolled himself. We asked how long he'd been smoking and he said "Maybe forty-five years." I said, "Mr. Helms, why do you want to quit smoking? It seems to me you might not have the same concern about sickness that some others might have—and you've gone so long without a problem."

He squinted his eyes and said, "Ma'am, I want to quit smoking because of my old lady." I said that was noble, but unacceptable. We insist that smokers enter the program with a selfishly personal desire to quit, rather than doing it for their spouse or someone else.

"I've a good personal reason, all right," he said. "I'm sick and tired of hearing her laugh and taunt me every morning when I cough my guts out." He paused and then said, "If I stop smoking my cough will get better, won't it?"

Sure enough, Mr. Helms's cough disappeared within one week after he quit smoking. And he brought his "old lady" to graduation. She wasn't so bad—but she certainly had no sympathy for all us damn fools who didn't know how to quit by ourselves and had to come to socialize to do it.

Incidentally, Mr. Helms was retired and bored. Shortly after he completed the course he dropped in to see me and announced he had gotten to think about what we said about living fully and he felt so great that he found himself a job as a watchman. He looked about twenty years younger.

Next rationalization: "If it really did harm people, the government would prohibit smoking." The beginning of this chapter should have stripped away that rationalization.

"I've got to die of something—I might as well die happy with my cigarettes!" Let's get back to that one.

Oh, yes, that's a wonderful old workhorse of a rationalization. It sounds good—but unfortunately the game isn't played that way. One usually doesn't just up and die from cancer or emphysema or heart disease. Cancer is swift and painful—often less than six months. The others are slow and painful. One can be a cardiac cripple or a respiratory invalid for years and years. And you won't die "happily"—it'll be torture.

But that's not fair. I am not trying to scare you or help you decide to quit because of fear. Those things didn't help me and I'm convinced they won't help you. (It's wonderful reinforcement *after* you've quit smoking. You can look back and say, "Whew— I'm glad I don't have to worry about that anymore!")

But there is an important point to be made about this rationalization. It's not a question of how much sooner you might die, or even how. The point is whether you want to dull the quality of your life while you're alive. More important than dying is how you live while you are alive—the quality of your life. It's not a question of living longer, or dying ten years sooner. The fact is, you don't lose your life at the end: you're losing it now. If you're smoking at 30, you have the same health and vitality as a man of 40; if you're 40 you are functioning like a man of 50. It's not a matter of chance, like cancer or emphysema. *It really is happening now.* You'll know it when you quit, because your body will restore itself quickly, and your vitality, color and energy will return in bursts. Try it—you'll like it!

And how about "If I didn't smoke, I'd be very nervous." We've already seen that because of the chemical reaction, the opposite is true. Refer to Chapter 5 again. In addition, when you correctly stop smoking, you walk away from a certain hysteria. Some of us exhibit it externally and some feel it only internally. But that hysteria disappears when you've stopped, and in its place comes a certain serenity, calmness. A lot of ex-smokers tell us how calm they have felt since they stopped smoking, and many of them say, "Since I quit smoking I haven't lost my temper or my 'cool.'"

That's due not only to the elimination of the nicotine stimulant, and a decrease in caffeine intake, but also to a strong new sense of self-confidence. When you quit smoking you have done something measurable. It's not like learning to read faster or to speak more effectively in front of people. Those are matters of degree. When you quit smoking, you have done something that changes your life measurably. And you can be very proud of yourself. What's more, you did it yourself. You may attend a program to get direction, but in the final analysis, only you quit.

Let's go on with our rationalizations. Here's one that almost every woman has used: "If I quit smoking I will gain weight!" I've long suspected this was fostered by the tobacco industry. And people's worst fears are supported by stories of people who gained tons when they quit smoking. It reminds me of all the horror stories I heard about labor and childbirth before I had our first child. Many women had felt obliged to tell me, in minute detail, all the worst. Fortunately, my obstetrician, Dr. Warner, was alert to the danger such fishwifery could cause and made me promise not to listen to anyone but him about what to expect. He trained me in a natural-childbirth method, and I participated in each of our four deliveries—with no horror stories. Just great pleasure at being awake and in attendance at the delivery of each of our babies.

So, in like manner, the story goes out on the "wire service" from smoker to smoker that a condition of stopping smoking is gaining weight. It simply isn't true. There's not some mystical force that connects a circuit in your system to cigarettes and that, when disconnected, causes a weight gain. I didn't gain when I finally stopped. I held my same weight for about six years after I stopped, with no thought of diet or restrictions. Now, in my advancing years, and my more sedentary life as a business executive, I *have* put on weight. But it was certainly not a result of quitting smoking. And my story isn't unique.

When I had tried quitting before I followed a method similar to the one I spell out in this book, I had tried to substitute anything I could put into my mouth, and I would gain weight. Fast. I'd have the lovely excuse I was looking for to start again. "Heavens," I'd say, "I'd rather die from a lung disease than from obesity." Of course people gain weight if, when they quit smoking, they start stuffing their mouths with everything that isn't nailed down. If I tell you that you should attend to your mouth to satisfy its need for oral satisfaction, you must understand that it shouldn't be with the wrong kind of food. You could chew on ginger root or a clove, or some other non–habit-forming item. It's better not to start with gum or candy, which would only give you another habit to deal with later on, and maybe cavities in addition.

Some people experience a change in their metabolism. Which is great. Your body becomes much more efficient and utilizes the food more efficiently. Some people need less food than formerly —or they need more exertion to burn up the same amount of food intake. Fortunately, when you stop smoking and have more energy and vitality, you will want to do more physical things— increase the amount of time you spend on the courts, or begin swimming again, or take to walking briskly. It's more inviting now that you don't start coughing the moment you breathe deeply.

The question of weight is in your hands. If you want an excuse to start smoking again, allow the fat to build up. But remember, you'd have to weigh about 125 pounds over your present weight to do as much damage to your heart as you do by smoking only one pack of cigarettes a day. And when you quit smoking you can do almost anything, so losing weight is a good next goal.

Here's another old one: "What good is quitting? I inhale more junk in the air because of all the pollution. A little more won't make much difference!" That's an easy balloon to shoot down. Try this test. Take a clean white handkerchief and walk out into the most polluted area you can think of. Take a deep breath. Hold the handkerchief in front of your mouth and blow out through the handkerchief. Now, light a cigarette, and take a deep drag. Before exhaling, place the handkerchief in front of your mouth again, and blow through it. The black spot of "tar" from your cigarette will demonstrate to you the matter of dilution and filtration. Polluted air, although it's not pure and healthful, is much more diluted than "straight smoke" from your cigarette. There's no contest. You really don't have to go to all this trouble. If you smoke filter-tips, tear one apart after you've smoked it and examine the gook that's collected in the filter. And that's only part of it. The rest is still in your lungs.

How about this one? "I smoke because it tastes good." Yes, I eat pecan pie because it tastes good—but by golly, if I ate twenty or thirty pieces of pecan pie a day, I'd vomit from here to Hackensack. We've already explored enjoyment and you have observed yourself smoking and found just how many and which cigarettes give you pleasure. Now I suggest you do the same for taste. Observe yourself smoking and see how many cigarettes—*no, how many puffs*—taste good to you.

And what about the mornings after, when you've smoked a lot of cigarettes at a party or a meeting? I remember smoking cigarettes that tasted foul, and I remember mornings when my mouth tasted like the bottom of a birdcage. I can't tell you what things taste like to you and what you consider a good taste. You are examining your smoking conditions with a high degree of personal honesty. I expect your answer to how many puffs taste good each day will fall in the same range with the answers of our regular smokEnders who search for taste. Frequently *none* have tasted good.

If you're getting more eager to quit smoking, I suggest you do something to change the conditions in your mouth regarding taste. Milk isn't generally considered a good partner for a cigarette; it doesn't enhance the taste of cigarettes. Find things that are opposite in relation to your taste for a cigarette. Avoid the "ham-and-eggs" combinations, such as coffee and a cigarette. End your meals and snacks with something that doesn't naturally lead to a cigarette.

The importance of this exercise is to give you some awareness of your ability to control your smoking "environment." Once you realize you can interfere with many of the conditions of smoking in rather pleasant ways, you will look forward to quitting as a hopeful challenge rather than a hopeless battle.

"It's my buddy!" This is a pet rationalization of most smokers —and for good reason. Cigarette ads direct their message to this concept to a large degree. They know we have developed a close relationship with our cigarettes and our brand. Not long ago a major advertising campaign touted "Me and my ————"—the implication being that a smoker and his "buddy" could lick the world alone and he didn't need any other (human) relationship. I don't know whether it sold cigarettes, but it imprinted the idea strongly in a lot more minds. (I discuss the effect of cigarette ads in Chapter 7.)

If you're anxious to "disconnect" yourself from another subtle connection to the habit, examine your "friendship" toward your cigarettes and your brand. Ask, "What kind of friend would 'control' me—and perhaps cripple or kill me?" Begin to change your view of Old Buddy to *a friend who betrayed me.* If that's still too strong for you, think of it as an old flame from your youth, someone you lost interest in who chases you and coaxes you to return.

This thinking should lead you to the best possible attitude after you quit smoking. Indifference! *You should not feel that you've given up something precious, but simply that you've lost interest in smoking.*

And finally: "I can't imagine myself not smoking. It's part of me." This is probably the only valid statement in the lot: most of us started so young we don't know what it's like to be an adult nonsmoker. We have no idea what capability an undrugged adult body has, in endurance, energy or sustained good health. Nor our minds. We can't really know how much we limit our thinking processes because we don't know what our full capability is.

I was impressed with the observations of a former smoker who received his doctorate from MIT many years ago and has been highly successful in his field. He wrote to me about a year after he had quit smoking, "I have discovered that I labored under about a 25% handicap while I was smoking; now, having quit smoking and dealing with the same theoretical and practical problems, I realize that I am able to comprehend, reason and calculate much more clearly and rapidly. I regret the years spent working at less than my fullest capacity."

And this is true of cigar and pipe smokers, too: the same effect of carbon monoxide upon the brain which reduces peak performance. Because it doesn't matter what you smoke—cigars, pipes, high- or low-tar cigarettes, lettuce leaves, cellulose or shoe leather. They all produce carbon monoxide as an end product of combustion. As you draw in the smoke, you subject yourself to substantial doses of carbon monoxide. There's no way to escape it.

That brings up another form of rationalization. Pipe and cigar smokers often say, "I'm safe because I don't inhale." Or "Cigars and pipe smoking aren't harmful—it's cigarettes that do the damage." Unfortunately, both statements are cover-ups. Pipe and cigar smokers, when reading this book, should translate the word "cigarette" to "pipe" or "cigar," because all I have said about cigarette smokers applies to cigar and pipe smokers too. In fact, cigar and pipe smokers use smoking in additional ways to insulate themselves—and they have an exceedingly strong view of themselves as smokers. It seems a great part of their person. Truly a physical extension of themselves.

Okay, smoking seems to be part of you. There's nothing else you do with such frequency. Nothing. And your mental image of yourself is as a smoker. You picture yourself attached to a cigarette just as you picture yourself with a nose attached to your face. That's what must change. You must be able to see yourself without a cigarette before you can begin to disconnect from the habit.

From this point on, I'll ask you to try to imagine yourself as a nonsmoker. In your mind's eye, see yourself "clean"—without a cigarette in your hand or in an ashtray near you. Observe people you admire who don't smoke, and begin to model your mental image of yourself along their lines. Begin to look forward to a time when cigarettes don't dominate your existence; when you can come and go anywhere, anytime, without considering whether you have enough cigarettes, if you'll be permitted to smoke, if you'll offend anyone; and especially when you can say to yourself, "I'm no longer controlled by that tube of chopped-up vegetables wrapped in paper; I am my own person.

Visualize yourself as a free person.

seven

CIGARETTE ADVERTISING: REWARD PARODIES

Let's look at the cigarette ads from the tobacco industry's point of view. The cigarette companies have really done a superb job of marketing their product. Can you imagine persuading sixty to seventy million people to do something that costs money; that's kind of dirty; that makes them smell bad; that usually offends friends and relatives; that causes gagging and coughing, slows them down, is in general a pretty messy nuisance and might kill them?

I give the tobacco industry and its advertising agencies credit for doing a tremendous job. I don't like what they do, because I've seen the wrong end of it for many years—early deaths; the pain and the anguish smokers experience from knowing their suffering has been self-inflicted.

But it's not my role to hassle the tobacco industry or act like "hatpin Annie"—we in smokEnders are not vindictive and we're not interested in wasting effort and energy on vendettas. The objective is to help people break free from the smoking habit if they have decided they'd like to quit. This book is intended to help you consider quitting and to help you gear up for action. But it's important to have a good, clear view of the propaganda and not continue to let the ads reach you even subliminally.

I can hear you say, "Oh, the ads don't get me. I'm not moved by them; I don't even see them, really. I'm too sharp for that!" Sure you are, except that I don't believe it because I said it myself too, and I was in the advertising business as a young career woman and prided myself on being astute about advertising messages. And yet the ads influenced me, though I didn't know to what length and depth until I stopped smoking.

So let's talk about the approach the tobacco industry took to lead us into its domain. Let's turn the tables by using the ads to get disengaged from the habit.

Their approach, for the longest time, was "Reward yourself. Treat yourself to something special." "For a treat instead of a treatment" was no accident. Advertising copywriters understand human nature—and human needs. Our need for recognition is fully discussed in Chapter 5. Go back over it and think about ways to reward yourself other than by smoking cigarettes.

The next exercise, something you'll enjoy, is rather like exorcising a devil. If that sounds dramatic, forgive me, but I know how strongly the cigarette ads are imprinted upon your mind, whether or not you know it yet. Let me try to make my point.

Suppose smoking were required by a government decree, like taxes or payroll reports. Can you imagine the uproar? There would be a rebellion. Not just because it violated our rights and forced us to do something against our will, but because it is such a dangerous and disgusting activity. And no amount of advertising would persuade us that it could be good for us, that it would improve the economy, that we might learn to like it.

So what has given us all the idea that smoking is a pleasure, that it creates a desirable image? *We were programmed*. It hasn't always been so. Cigarettes were a minor commodity until World War I, when they were issued to soldiers as a gesture of kindness. But they didn't gain public acceptance on a large scale until years later, when some brilliant advertising minds realized they had to aim at the "beautiful" people. Instead of directing their advertising efforts toward the tobacco-chewing crowd from which their customers were largely drawn, they consciously and vigorously portrayed smoking as "smart" and sophisticated, something done by the much-admired "upper class." In terms of changing public opinion, the new advertising direction was a huge success. The rest is history. The ads struck the nerve, were right on target. People forced themselves to smoke since it was so "in." The ads kept telling our parents that they couldn't make it unless they smoked. And they smoked in great numbers.

I'm going to tell you how to translate the ads so that they work *for* you instead of against you. The early ads took a slick, sophisticated approach; the current ones show machismo and "cool."

Here's how to read the ads. It's something we teach in the smokEnders program, which is fun and effective. You'll soon get the hang of it and never again be subject to their subtle manipulation. What we do is parody the ads. If you change one thing, it will change the whole meaning. A favorite of mine is the ad that shows a rather angry-looking young man with his shirt open to his navel, a neck chain and the proper accessories of his generation that represent "cool." The copy announces, "I like the box!" This can be read in several ways—take your choice. Either the boy prefers to smoke the box or he is referring to an off-color meaning of "box." In either case, he's not selling cigarettes. What about the fellow who's been scuba-diving with heavy equipment? He's sitting on the edge of a boat and reaching for a cigarette. This should read "I can't dive 'cause I smoke; just don't have the wind." Or how about the young lady who says, "If it weren't for ———, I wouldn't smoke"? Except, when she runs out of that brand, she'll smoke "Others" brand—anything else she can get her hands on. She's hooked!

And Mr. Cowboy. Why that should sell cigarettes is hard to understand unless you catch what underlies it: ego, machismo, toughness, "cool." Change the copy to read "Come to Cancer Country." This is what a British TV outfit did recently. It asked permission to film the famous cowboys for a documentary on effective advertising. It interviewed cowboys who had been stricken with lung cancer, emphysema and other smoking-induced diseases. The program was a knockout, though very embarrassing to the company.

Right now there are a great number of low-tar cigarettes on the market. Their copy implies that they are "safer." But safer than what? Read their ads and laugh. Each one promises less tar than the next, though *Reader's Digest* proclaims that low-tar brands produce considerably more poisonous gas than regular brands. And one new ad asserts that brand ———— has less poisonous gas than other brands. Read these ads as a confession from the tobacco industry. "These are *less* damaging than other brands . . ." How funny that they have been so caught up in the race for sales—with their internal bickering—that they're hanging their dirty laundry out in public.

I'm reminded of the old ads—when cigarettes were first found to have a link with cancer. The ads tumbled off the presses declaring that each brand was "less irritating . . ." or "cooler on the throat . . ." or contained a more effective filter which sifted out a lot of the dangerous elements.

Let's face it. There is nothing good one can really say about cigarettes in print. When you take time out to think about the words the copywriters use and not the pictures, you soon realize that they can't think of anything good to say (without breaking the law).

Have you seen the ad about the man who has just won $25,000, has poured a bucket of champagne over his head and is certainly not going to follow all that with a "boring" cigarette? You have to picture him lighting up, fireworks coming out of his cigarette, as a brass band plays "The Stars and Stripes Forever." Well, you have to admit, that would be exciting.

Or you see a picture of an intense young man with beautiful hair and a beard, looking at you straight on and saying, "If I'm going to smoke, I'm going to do it right." Your imagination can really take off on that one. "First, I must extract the cigarette from the pack without bending it; then I must be sure not to put the tobacco end in my mouth and light the filter tip; and I certainly want to be careful not to singe my beard. Today I'm going to do it right."

Do smokers always dress in color-coordinated outfits of the latest style, and wrinkleless? Are smokers' hair perfectly groomed, nails gorgeously manicured? Most ads show us smokers who are youthful, slender, with a glow of good health and well-being; laughing, horsing around in the water (how do they keep their cigarettes dry?), having loads of fun. How many of us really look like that? But another approach makes the smoker look foolish (but loyal)—the optimists who walk into things and break their cigarettes, the loyalists with blackened eyes, the men with the holes in their shoes.

You should pay attention to what is really being said. Many of the words are what is known in the trade as "weasel words": words that are evasions or retreats; words that either mean nothing or imply something that isn't true. One of the big weasel words is "helps," which in fact means aids or assists. What the ad is saying, as it uses that word, is that the product doesn't actually *do* what it claims to do, it only *partially* does it. "The filter *helps* trap gas." The ad neglects to tell you the names of the gases because they are lethal poisons, and you probably won't want to smoke a poisonous product. Poisons like carbon monoxide (you know, like from out of the back of your car?) and hydrogen cyanide are examples.

"Like" is another "weasel word" that confuses. *Like* invokes comparison—something may seem to be one thing, but in fact really isn't. "Draws like a gentle breeze." Have you ever drawn in a gentle breeze?

And what about "taste," which is a purely subjective daydream of the copywriter's? Who can say that a cigarette has the "taste" of "iced lightning" unless perhaps you've tasted iced lightning. Then there are "smooth taste" and "cool taste," the "taste of fresh menthol" (another ingredient that is causing suspicion these days)—how, one wonders, does that compare with *stale* menthol?

There are the taste of adventure, the taste of all outdoors, a "taste that is very real" (is there a taste that is very phony?). And why all these euphemisms? Does anyone ever say a cigarette tastes like tobacco? No, because as I said before, cigarettes do taste lousy most of the time, and if the ads admitted that cigarettes tasted like tobacco, who would want to smoke them?

If one were to substitute the word "cigarettes" for the name of a specific brand that is heavily promoted, the copy would read, "If it weren't for cigarettes, I wouldn't smoke."

We often imagine how cigarette commercials might appear if they were still permitted on television. David Ballantine, a friend with a lively imagination, dreamed up this scenario: An ambulance is seen racing through the night—lightning, thunder, flashing red lights, sudden stop in front of a massive building. Attendants run around to the back of the ambulance. Doors are flung open. An unusually beautiful blond woman is lifted out on a stretcher. She is wearing expensive jewelry and is covered with a gold-lamé blanket. Camera pans to front of building. ". . . Memorial Cancer Institute" is visible on the stone lintel above the door. Voice over: "You've come a long way, baby." Realizing that there is nothing good to say about cigarettes can make ad watching a self-reinforcing activity.

It is a most curious fact that cigarette manufacturers are now obliged by law to spend 2 percent of their advertising space and advertising dollars to warn you off their product! "Warning: The Surgeon General has determined that cigarette smoking is dangerous to your health" must be prominently displayed on ads, billboards and packaging. Is there another consumer product that says "this product is dangerous to your health" that we would buy? Butter? A mattress? A child's toy? How about dog food? Would we ever buy a can of dog food that stated unequivocally on the label, "Warning, this food is bad for the health of your dog"?

It is also interesting that at the last count, there were 145 varieties of cigarettes on the American domestic market, and nearly all of them are manufactured by six major companies. It's fairly obvious that the company that makes the best ads—not the best cigarettes—wins.

At smokEnders we point out that ads don't really influence which cigarette you smoke. How many times have you as a smoker actually changed your brand over the past twenty years? Once? Perhaps twice? Many ads imply that smoking a certain brand of cigarette will add tremendous sex appeal, because those are the ads that have the best-looking models, who exude sensuality and suggest that all you need to emulate them is to smoke their brand. How much sex appeal can you have if your hair and body smell of stale smoke, if you have nicotine-stained teeth and fingers, if your breath reeks? There is also evidence that smoking inhibits sexual performance. Our graduates have often alluded to the fact that stopping smoking had had an opposite effect. *Subliminal Seduction* by Wilson Bryan Key points out that cigarette ads are filled with sexual imagery and phallic symbols. The consumer is supposed to be defenseless against such enticements. Still, smoking a cigarette waxes pale in comparison with the real thing.

Cigarette advertising campaigns of the nineteen-thirties and forties seem primitive in the light of what we know today about smoking. It was a time when the medical profession was somewhat naive about the dangers of smoking and doctors were even known in some cases to *recommend* smoking to patients who were nervous, or who wanted to lose weight. Cigarette advertising went to great lengths to assume a medical seal of approval, figuratively speaking. One brand actually claimed statistically that "20,679 Physicians say" that that particular brand was "less irritating because 'It's toasted' " (the advertiser's quotes around 'It's toasted,' immediately lead to suspicion). Then the copy went on to say that this toasting was "Your Throat Protection against irritation and against cough," that "Toasting removes dangerous irritants that cause throat irritation and coughing." This was before filter tips, an innocent age. One could, in any event, thus naturally assume that if your doctor smoked a particular cigarette, then it really had to be good for you.

Approach cigarette ads with a fresh point of view. You'll probably find that they will help you get ready to stay off cigarettes. When you read the ad that asks, "If smoking isn't a pleasure, why bother?" you may say, "You know, it *isn't* a pleasure; I guess I *won't* bother!" Another connection disconnected!

If you want to do it right, begin tearing out ads and leave them around until you have a good idea of how to change the meaning. If there are children around, they do marvels with this. I remember one time our son Peter, then about 10, found a typical ad of the lovely young lady sitting by a cool pool, looking fresh and pure, holding a cigarette in her hand, waiting expectantly for Mr. Wonderful, who was emerging from the background. Ah, what promises of joy and pleasure were implied! Peter destroyed the image with one move of his pencil. He blackened one of her front teeth.

When you have created a good parody, you might hang it on your refrigerator for the whole family to enjoy. It does a good job in helping youngsters learn to "read" the ads. Satire is a marvelous tool to prevent children from starting to smoke.

eight

CHANGING OTHER HABITS: WHAT ABOUT ALCOHOL, COKE, PEPSI, COFFEE AND MARIJUANA?

Invariably, smokEnder graduates ask, "Now that I've kicked that cigarette habit, would there be any risk if I smoked 'grass' ('pot,' 'dope,' 'a joint'—or, by any other name, marijuana)?" They're asking the question not relative to the health risks of smoking pot, but to the risk of resuming smoking cigarettes.

Of course, it's sensible to avoid any possibility of resuming smoking once one has finally quit. So, ideally, we should sidestep alcohol, too, and coffee, Coke/Pepsi and almost any other substance that acts as a "trigger" for a cigarette. I've met hardly any smokers who haven't been tied to the combination of cigarette-and-coffee; cigarette-and-liquor; cigarette-and-Coke. We have records of smokers who have consumed up to thirty cups of coffee a day or about twenty bottles of Coke a day while they were smokers—and when they stopped smoking their caffeine intake dropped dramatically; and many near-alcoholics have reported they reduced their alcohol intake considerably, in some cases totally. Stopping smoking, they also broke the conditioned-response "command" and found they didn't need to drink coffee, Coke or alcohol as much as before.

In addition, because they weren't drugged by nicotine and all the gases which slowed them down mentally and physically while they were smoking, they found they didn't need the lift or release which those cigarette "companions" seemed to offer. In fact, the sense of being turned on is remarkably strong when one stops smoking correctly, well prepared to walk coolly and graciously away from the habit, so we don't require other means to get turned on as much as when we smoked tobacco.

But life is not perfect, and sometimes we need a kick. So for those who want to smoke a joint now and then after they've kicked the habit, we caution them to avoid it until they are well away from the cigarette habit—until they have come to enjoy not-smoking and view not-smoking as a pleasure which they wouldn't want to give up. Once that attitude is achieved, it's reasonable to assume that one could smoke a joint with sufficient disassociation from the cigarette condition so that it wouldn't trigger off a desire for a regular cigarette. That's the real problem. It's also a matter of resolve.

In order to have quit successfully, you will have convinced yourself that you really wanted to quit; that there was something in it for you personally and that you're worth it. This resolve becomes stronger and stronger as you successfully pass by each condition that used to remind you of a cigarette. Your self-esteem increases and, with it, your resolve.

It takes considerable practice to become an experienced ex-smoker just as it took practice to become an experienced smoker. During the practice stage of not-smoking—for a period of time after you've quit—your resolve is vulnerable. You might even occasionally forget the reason you wanted to quit. And then, there are times when your resolve is softened by chemical forces—alcohol, for instance.

Let's look at the effects of alcohol on your system when you are a smoker and when you are a nonsmoker. Since your body maintains a level of nicotine (generally a stimulant) while you support the cigarette habit, the effect of alcohol (generally a depressant) is reduced. When you stop smoking, alcohol functions at full strength and packs a much stronger wallop. (This could be a nice additional reason for wanting to quit smoking: you will need less to achieve the same feeling. This observation has been reported to us by numerous smokEnder graduates.)

Here's the peril: When you have a drink, it softens the resolve. You adopt an "I don't give a damn" attitude, and the chances of reaching for a cigarette are vastly increased. I'd be willing to bet that more people start smoking again because they were caught off guard by alcohol's new kick, or pot's ability to "take the edge off things," than for almost any other reason.

So the answer to "What about marijuana now that I've kicked the cigarette habit?" is, if you want to protect your precious new habit of not-smoking, steer clear of marijuana for a while. And by all means go easy on the alcohol. You'll soon find you really don't need to drink so much or so often because you don't have a cigarette that needs a companion—a drink. And because you will have come to realize that you don't need to follow old patterns just from habit. Stopping smoking is a catalyst for getting out of other ruts.

In fact, one of the pleasantest results of quitting smoking was reported by Greenwich, Connecticut, advertising executive. He had completed the smokEnder course about six months before. "Dear Mrs. Rogers," he wrote, "I can't begin to tell you how much your program has done for me. Not only have I quit smoking very comfortably, which I thought was totally impossible for a person in my position and industry, but I have rearranged some other very important conditions in my life."

He described some rather touching personal situations in his life, including a drinking ritual. Without ever questioning why, he had had a couple of drinks at lunch and three martinis before dinner. He had steadily increased his alcohol consumption over the years. Then, in his late 40's, he had observed that life had taken a downturn; things weren't exciting lately. He had begun to ask himself that question many people ask as they lift up their heads and look around after about forty years of pressing on through school and marriage and a career: "Is this all there is?"

"I found my life was becoming a boring routine. Rat race all day—same problems, different people. At night, I'd generally get home for a late dinner, after a couple of relaxing drinks, and stumble into bed so I could get up to go through the same routine in the morning. I'd say to myself, 'What's it all about?' "

Then he described the change he had made in his life-style, after his smokEnder Moderator had taught him to determine if his routines might be an impediment now.

"That silly little 'ham story' you use in the program to persuade us to look at our life-style and patterns objectively really did the trick for me," he wrote. "I recognized that I could change much about my routine if I chose to. So I did. I realized I didn't need those drinks at lunch anymore. The reason I got into that routine in the first place was because as a young man at my first job in New York, having a cocktail at lunch was a sign of 'belonging' to the fast-moving, sophisticated advertising clique. Everyone did it. The ritual. A vodka gimlet or a vodka martini at lunch was big stuff. (The reason it had to be vodka was because it left no odor on my breath.) Ordering two drinks at lunch took some years of development and signified another level of achievement for us. It let the world know that we could hold our liquor—two cocktails would 'snogger' ordinary types. And it expressed our financial status to the world. We could afford to squander our salary; two cocktails were expensive for a file clerk but not for a rising young executive.

"Then after I married, Madeleine and I followed the script of the scene as we had read it and seen it portrayed in plays, movies and books. It was another note of sophistication to have cocktails ready when I came home from the office. At first it got in the way of doing the things I looked forward to doing when I got home —like mowing the lawn or finishing the antique chest we had bought on our honeymoon. Soon I learned to stop promising myself I'd get things done in the evenings. That's what Saturdays are for, they told me at the office.

"And soon Madeleine became busy with the children, so we

added a second cocktail to the routine to give her a bit more time to get dinner ready. Eventually it became three before dinner for me, because I'd stop at the Biltmore for a drink with Harvey before we took our separate trains at Grand Central. Dinner was always late, so I had extra time.

"And my evenings were all the same, unless we had friends over. A couple of drinks, a late dinner, watch the news on TV and then to bed.

"I simply accomplished nothing between leaving the office and going to bed. And I always complained that I didn't have time to get everything done that was pressing me.

"Sure, I carried home a briefcase full of work, but unless there was a critical deadline, I rarely worked in the evening.

"So when Ruth Sussman, my moderator, suggested we take a cold, hard look at our patterns and routines and see if we had created some 'self-imposed jails and ruts,' I thought about that old wooden chest I had started to refinish. And I thought about the wasteland of my evenings, and I understood what Ruth was aiming at.

"As a result of quitting smoking, I've also cut down on my alcohol intake and have added four hours a day to my existence, because I don't have three cocktails before dinner. As a result, we have an earlier dinner and I'm raring to go instead of being heavy-headed and tired. Now I look forward to the evenings as a time to spend on things I enjoy.

"I wish someone had told me years ago that I didn't have to play out the scenario of the Hollywood/Broadway stereotype of a sophisticate. So your program did far more for me than simply help me kick the habit. It improved the quality of my life beyond belief, for which I extend my most sincere appreciation."

Here's the "ham story" which influenced our friend (and many, many others who've taken a cue from it):

A newly married couple decided to invite their parents to dinner as their first try at having company. They planned and shopped very earnestly, and then the proud young husband watched his bride prepare the meal. They had decided on baked ham, and after she had completed preparing it for the roasting pan, she sliced a chunk off one end and put it in the roasting pan next to the ham.

"Why did you do that, honey?" he asked.

"Oh," she said, "I honestly don't know. That's the way my mother always did it."

Perplexed, he asked his mother-in-law at dinner that evening, "Why did you always cut the end off the ham?"

"You know, I really don't know, come to think of it. But my mother always did it, and I never thought too much about it," she said.

The young husband was curious, and the next time they called on Grandma he remembered to ask her why she had cut the end off the ham. He wondered if it was a religious custom or had something to do with flavor.

"Good Lord, no," she said. "I cut the end off the ham because my roasting pan wasn't big enough."

Alcohol: Here's a suggestion for decreasing the amount of alcohol you consume without feeling deprived. Water it down. Whatever it is you drink (except beer, of course), you can add more mixer or soda or ice. When the day comes that you quit smoking, you won't have *two* big things to deal with. Also, one of the bonuses of stopping smoking is that you'll get a bigger kick from the same amount of alcohol.

Coffee: This is an interesting side condition. Our consumption of coffee is related directly to the number of cigarettes we smoke. So when we quit we discover that we have considerably reduced our coffee drinking, and not only are we less keyed up, our pocketbooks are fatter! The price of coffee has soared to something like $4 a pound. Also, you will save a considerable amount of time. Following the well-described routine of your day (and that of *most* smokers), you know there's a lot of stopping for coffee. One of our first members, Marilyn Durham, who now lives in Oregon, described her attachment to coffee while she smoked. I believe she drank thirty cups of coffee a day: she had a fifteen-cup coffee-pot in which she brewed coffee twice each day. After she comp-leted the seminar, not only had she quit smoking and cut down her coffee to about five cups a day, but she had a lot more time."In fact," she said, "I feel like somebody took the pressure off my life. Everything is calmer and less frenzied. I seem to get my work done in half the time and still have time to loaf or do the things I enjoy without feeling like my work is backing up on me."

The problem of coffee nerves disappears, and with it go all the stalling and indecision represented by the coffee ritual. Here's how it works. (I call it the Sunday-morning planning session, because that's how it was with me.) Sunday morning: We look forward to a day of pleasure and doing all those good things we've waited for all week. Everybody has high hopes for the day. First, though, we have to have breakfast talk over coffee about what we're going to do. Each cigarette demands another cup of coffee, and each cup of coffee requires another cigarette. The discussion is prolonged "just until I finish my cigarette," or "just until I finish this cup of coffee." The two never quite get into sync.

The morning is wasted, the kids are cranky because they are anxious to do whatever they had hoped to do with the family and by the time we get our act together, most of the precious day is gone.

A lot of the Monday-morning blues is a hangover of a disap-pointing Sunday.

Many of us repeat the ritual in miniature each time we stop for a coffee break, or a Coke or a cup of tea. It seems to be worse for those at home than for those in an office. We did a random sampling of smokers to determine how much time they spent drinking coffee each day. They were asked to list the time they spent drinking coffee and working simultaneously, and the amount of time they spent drinking coffee as a means of taking a break or socializing. Not counting breakfast, lunch and dinner coffee, the response ranged from thirty minutes to two hours a day. Measuring this against the habits of nonsmokers, we discovered that the latter spent about 55 percent less of their time drinking coffee for a "break."

There's a whole area of habits to explore in an effort to understand yourself in order to get ready to quit smoking successfully. That's the whole question of other drugs which you may be introducing into your system each day, not really thinking about the problems they create. Coffee is one of them. Or a "nondrug," as Edward Brecher, in his book *Licit and Illicit Drugs*, (Consumer Reports–Little, Brown), classifies caffeine. "Nonmedically, caffeine is the most widely used central nervous system stimulant, popular in the form of coffee, tea, cocoa and 'cola' drinks. Heavy users of these beverages report tolerance, physical dependence and withdrawal symptoms, and craving."

Many people are surprised to learn that their friendly tea and cola are also laced with caffeine, especially since they offer those drinks to children as an acceptable beverage. It's something of a shock to learn that you've been offering children a rather strong drug, a stimulant. Generally, I had been given tea or cocoa to quiet me or to relax me if I had a cold or was recovering from a fever or a childhood illness.

As for cola drinks—which aren't viewed as therapeutically as tea and cocoa—caffeine is the kicker there too. But never mind trying to decide whether you must abstain from all pleasures if you quit smoking. The answer is no. I sincerely believe you should be able to quit smoking and simply disengage your smoking habit from your other habits without too much disturbance. In fact, in whatever form you take your caffeine, you should be very careful not to cut down too sharply too quickly, or you'll compound your withdrawal situation.

In the meantime, here are a couple of thoughts to help you out.

Substitute bouillon for several of the breaks. Keep a few packages in your pocket or your desk. I prefer the powdered kind in the foil packet. Very small. Very tasty. And it dissolves in hot water. When you feel like a good, hot pickup, try bouillon. It has helped a large number of smokers in the program. It contains protein, which gives you a boost, and it's soothing, rather than stimulating. Many of the brands contain sodium, so if you're on a limited diet, discuss it with your doctor.

The other suggestion is to be aware that coffee is a mild diuretic. If you cut down sharply, you might find yourself feeling bloated. Sometimes you retain fluid until the body makes the necessary adjustments to handle the fluid without benefit of caffeine. If you find you're feeling "swollen"—perhaps your rings feel tight, or your shoes—the cause might be your reduction in coffee. If that's the case, there's nothing to worry about because it will pass. You can help it along by eating such things as mushrooms, spinach or asparagus, which are natural diuretics. Or ask your doctor for a suggestion.

Cut down your caffeine intake slowly. Use milk, water or bouillon as an occasional substitute. Do something about fluid retention before it causes bad temper which could encourage you to quit trying to get out of your double trap.

If you seem particularly affected by sharp drops in your blood sugar, you should consider going all the way and "decaffeinating" yourself entirely. Use Sanka or any other decaf drink. Coffee takes you up and puts you down hard and fast. You'll feel better without coffee, more alive and peppy. Do it slowly; be kind to your body —it's the only one you have!

nine

ADDICTION

One remark common to all smokers is "But I enjoy smoking." Almost every smoker has said it. It's hardly surprising. Not only is it bound up in your right to choose how you live, but the implication is that you deserve some simple pleasures in life, and if smoking gives you pleasure, you don't have to deprive yourself of it. (You bet I understand. I made that remark thousands of times.)

Since nicotine is addictive, since the body requires that a certain level must be maintained in the bloodstream, you become uncomfortable when you've gone beyond your normal time for another dose. Usually you react by reaching automatically for another cigarette. You've quickly added another shot of nicotine, so all's well.

Let's think of the times when you've run out of cigarettes. Perhaps it was Sunday morning, after you had had a gang over the night before. After the initial panic, and after you've hunted the house for a hidden pack, and been reduced to retrieving butts, you become aware of some strong physical signals from your body. At first, that vague discomfort in your gut becomes a kind of twitchy uneasiness. Soon you start feeling sweaty, cranky, maybe headachy, downright mean. Although you've probably promised yourself you'd finish dressing, have breakfast and do some routine chores before going to the store for cigarettes, you find yourself driving or running to the store, grabbing a pack, wolfing down the first drag and feeling some sense of peace again. "Ah, that's better. I really enjoy smoking. What a pleasure!"

What happened was that you were damned uncomfortable without a cigarette because of the lowered level of nicotine in your bloodstream. Lighting up relieved your discomfort, and you translated that to mean "enjoyed."

So here's what to do for the next three days: During one of those times you're forced to do without a cigarette past your dose requirement (Yes, dose. You need a "dose" of nicotine to maintain your comfort level just as a diabetic needs his insulin—except that when you stop smoking, the body becomes accustomed to doing without the nicotine and you can be comfortable without any additional doses), observe your sensations of discomfort.

List your sensations as they occur and note the amount of time between each sensation and a new one. A good list could easily run to about fifteen items.

(If you have already quit but want to disconnect the "enjoyment" connector, think about those times when you climbed the walls until you could get another cigarette.) Here are a few entries to help you get started:

Gnawing in the pit of the stomach.
Tightness in the throat, a sense of thickening.
Sweaty palms, leading to chills; later perspiration.
Rapid pulse.
Sharply increasing respiration.
Inability to concentrate on anything other than getting another
cigarette.

Now you have got hold of a big secret: nicotine is addictive—and you are addicted. If you can accept that, the rest is easy; the rest of the problem is manageable. It's not a matter of changing your character by willpower. I remember the relief I felt when I discovered this. In the old days, the popular belief was that cigarette smoking was "habituative," that nicotine didn't meet the criteria of addiction. (Smoking was just a nasty little habit.) I looked up the criteria of addiction in the "bible" of the pharmacologists, *The Pharmacological Basis of Therapeutics*, by Drs. Louis S. Goodman and Alfred Gilman, and it was clear that I was addicted. Their criteria for addiction are: measurable physical withdrawal symptoms and tolerance.

Why, I wondered, could I as a smoker recognize the condition as an addiction while the scientific and health community eschewed the designation? Years later I learned why. It was feared that to label smoking as an "addiction" would put it on the same level with heroin and imply equally severe detoxification suffering, which would so intimidate smokers that they'd be unable to quit.

In 1971, the Addiction Research Unit of the Institute of Psychiatry in London, which was established to study heroin addiction, took a long, hard look at cigarette smoking and adopted the view that nicotine *is* addictive. According to Dr. M. A. Hamilton Russell of the Institute, "It is far easier to become dependent on cigarettes than on alcohol or barbiturates," since the frequency of smoking far exceeds the intake of any other addictive substance used by man. "Most users of alcohol or sleeping tablets are able to limit themselves to intermittent use and to tolerate periods free of the chemical effect. If dependency occurs it is usually in a setting of psychological or social difficulty. Not so with cigarettes; intermittent or occasional use is a rarity—about 2 percent of smokers."

Dr. Russell added, ". . . in addition to psychological dependence, most cigarette smokers fulfill the criteria for physiological dependence (addiction), namely tolerance and physical withdrawal effects."

There is a disease, called Buerger's disease, which affects the circulation. The blood vessels that supply the extremities become constricted each time nicotine is inhaled. This can lead to gangrene. But the condition can reverse itself completely if the nicotine intake is completely cut off.

I remember a particularly moving incident some years ago. I was working late at the office when the phone rang. It isn't unusual for me to receive calls from smokers late at night asking for information about quitting. They take action impulsively when they get sufficiently disgusted with the habit. I expected the usual "I'm fed up with smoking; I just burned my blanket. How do I go about joining smokEnders?" This woman was crying. She begged me to help her husband. Right away. Here's what she told me:

"Jim and I have been married for about twelve years. We moved to this area so we could buy a little photography shop and have a country life for our children. We have three. Two boys, thirteen and eleven, and a girl, nine. Jim is the photographer. A good one. I do some photography, order materials and I'm the bookkeeper. We make a living and have been getting along okay. Then, last year, Jim got gangrene in his left hand. The doctor told him it would help if he quit smoking, but Jim didn't quit. He doctored for the hand, but it was no good. It hurt terrible. And it smelled fierce. He couldn't work, so I took over that too. And then the doctor told him he had to cut off his hand. So this year I've been helping Jim while he learned how to work with only his right hand."

She had trouble talking, because she was sobbing and trying to control herself.

"Then," she continued, "Jim began having trouble with one of the fingers on his right hand. He put off going to the doctor because he was scared, I guess. By the time he told me about the sore, it looked terrible. We went to the doctor, and he said, 'Jim, you must stop smoking or I'll have to remove this finger and maybe even the hand!' and Jim said 'How much time do I have to quit, Doc?' And the doctor said 'I can't give you more than five days, Jim.'

"So we went home and I pleaded with Jim to quit. He's only thirty-two and so wonderful and healthy otherwise. I guess I worked on his nerves, because he got angry at me and told me it was his life and he'd do what he wanted with it.

"I think he tried to quit for a day or so, because there weren't any cigarettes around one day. But yesterday, he was smoking again. I didn't know what to say or do. Today he's smoking just like always. When I asked him what we were going to do for a living if he had no hands, he said, and this is what made me crazy, 'That's not what worries me. I'm worried about how I'm going to smoke with no hands!'

"And tomorrow's the fifth day. Please, can you help him to stop smoking right away! I just saw your name in the newspaper."

So this is what experts and doctors see. They see the emphysema patient who can't breathe without a machine at regular intervals who puffs away on cigarettes in between; the heart-attack victim who knows his system has difficulty even in an oxygen tent and who starts smoking first chance he gets.

Why don't doctors routinely tell their patients to quit smoking, especially before the onset of disease caused by smoking? Let's have a little charity for the medical and dental professions. In the past, most physicians and dentists were convinced that smoking was detrimental to their patients' health. They learned in their pathology and physiology courses that nicotine was a lethal poison; commercial uses are for pesticides, for poisons and as a tanning agent on leather and hides (not to mention what it does to your face!); that it constricted the blood vessels so quickly and sharply as to cause a decrease in circulation which could be measured by a drop of up to 4°F. or more in skin temperature; that the effects of the constriction last from twenty to forty-five minutes after even one cigarette (American Heart Association); that in some cases circulation was so impaired as to cause Buerger's disease. Buerger's disease is called "smoker's disease" because it's so uncommon in nonsmokers. They also recognized that patients with bronchial afflictions suffered more serious and prolonged seizures if they smoked. It didn't take a lot of scientific study to observe that smokers with respiratory ailments coughed wildly with each puff of smoke into lungs already working hard to deal with minimal breathing.

Dentists too were aware of the increased difficulty smokers endure. They saw the harm smoking does in their patients—the diseased and flabby gums, the stained teeth and foul mouth odor, the precancerous lesions and horrifying cancers of the tongue, lips, cheeks and any other soft tissues of the oral cavity.

For a long time, they took a strong and honorable position: insist that the patient cease smoking immediately "or else." This was a little more difficult for the doctor who was a smoker, since the patient could make the observation that apparently the doctor wasn't too thoroughly convinced.

But the bigger problem arose when the patient left the doctor's office, vowing to quit, but found he was unable to deal with the problem without help. He climbed the walls. He was obsessed by the desire for a cigarette and he couldn't concentrate on anything else. He became wild and disagreeable, and so he returned to his doctor and said something like "Doc, I'd sure like to follow your instructions and quit smoking, but somehow I can't manage to do it without help. Give me a pill or something to help me."

Is there a pill for quitting smoking? There is not. If the doctor prescribed a nicotine substitute (lobeline sulfate/Nikoban), the patient soon found that he needed much more to help him than a tablet or chewing gum; if the doctor prescribed a tranquilizer, the patient relaxed so nicely he lost his resolve to quit and had a pleasant "I don't give a damn" attitude in its stead.

If the doctor was inclined to help by counseling, the patient required frequent appointments and undisturbed time, which was not only very costly but often ineffective, since medical and dental schools do not offer courses in "Breaking the Smoking Habit." (They have, of course, many courses in what to do about diseases that result from smoking.) So the addicts had very little to go on but their own instincts, judgment and conscientiousness.

My physician, a smoker, advised me to schedule appointments with a psychiatrist (then at $25 an hour) when I pleaded for help in quitting smoking. He felt I was unduly obsessed with quitting. He's since passed on. Heart attack. I don't think he made 60, but he had quit smoking shortly after I worked out the smokEnder method for myself.

The doctors learned that commanding a patient to stop smoking produced instant frustration, because the patient would quickly respond, "Okay, Doctor, but *how* should I quit? I've tried many times and I can't." The doctor had nothing to offer, so many doctors understandably skirted the issue. They'd say often, "Well, keep it in moderation." I asked my doctor, "What do you consider a moderate amount?" and he replied, "Oh, around a pack or so." I was happy about that for a while, because I had conned myself into believing that I smoked only a pack or so. (Really it was more like two packs a day, but I never kept a record and my purchases were very irregular, so I fooled myself for years.)

You'll see, as we progress through this book, how important the concept of addiction is to your success. For instance, when we discuss one of your pet rationalizations, "If I didn't smoke, I'd be very nervous and tense," you'll be able to clearly recognize the effect of the drug on your system and you'll be comforted to know you can function more effectively without it.

Let's look at the concern of the health agencies in regard to addiction. First, there's the matter of degree of addiction. Certainly, opium and heroin are much more powerful than nicotine.* Decreasing doses of heroin/opium per day are required to cause the desired effect. The body is more profoundly involved physically. Heartbeat and breathing rates are dramatically changed, while nicotine affects the bodily systems less violently. So the tortures of withdrawal, as depicted in movies and novels about the drug addict, are not nearly as bad for the smoker. But it can cause a smoker a fair amount of distress if he goes cold turkey. And it's

---

*As far as addiction is concerned, opium and heroin are far more intense and create a greater effect upon the mind and body; however, nicotine is a more potent poison. One drop in the eye of a rabbit kills it within seconds.

one of the reasons you've probably avoided quitting, even avoided
thinking about quitting. Each time you tried, you were probably
miserable and you succumbed to a cigarette. And now all you can
remember is the misery.

That's reasonable. Who likes to suffer? (This is an interesting
spiral: the thought of suffering as a result of quitting strengthens
your belief that you enjoy smoking. It could be a no-win situation.
But it's not, as you'll discover within the book.)

Here's an important fact, which should give you much support
when you're ready to quit: nicotine is out of your bloodstream
within three days after you stop smoking. (Unless, of course,
you're very sedentary or bedridden.) Think about that. Three days
and you're no longer craving the drug.

It's quite possible that you might have succeeded in quitting
smoking during a previous attempt if you'd known that. Getting
past the third day is a giant step toward success.

Knowing that addiction is one of the obstacles to success, you
can face up to it. It's not some vague bond that keeps you chained
to cigarettes. They contain a powerful drug, and it's better to
know what you're working with (or against).

Base your notions on stopping smoking on the fact that nicotine is addictive and that you can deal with it in solid, tangible
terms. How?

In smokEnders, we deal with it in an eight-week program, on
the basis of step-by-step instructions, which appear to work effectively only within the framework of the program, because there
is control and rapport between moderator and smoker. However,
here are some good and useful techniques you can use by yourself
to lower the level of nicotine in your bloodstream.

1. Step up your circulation by additional exercise. Jumping Jacks
   are the next-best thing to swimming for maximum results. I
   suggest you begin a regimen of increased exercise daily, with
   doctor's okay if you have any physical problems.
2. Begin drinking water regularly. Clear, cold water when you get
   up and before you go to sleep, and several times during the day.

It not only increases circulation, which in turn adds oxygen to your blood; it also improves your bowel functioning and digestive system, helps flush your kidneys and by cleansing the poisons out of your system more rapidly, makes you feel better. Now, there's a miracle drug.

3. You can reduce the amount of nicotine by changing brands, but this is dicey unless you're really going to stop within a very short time, because you'll smoke more to get the "right" amount of nicotine.

To sum up the arguments toward freeing yourself from the habit, remember that: nicotine is addictive, and its absence causes discomfort; lighting up is simply a relief of a self-induced discomfort.

Nicotine is poison. Can you ever again say, "But I *enjoy* smoking"? Say, instead, "I can do without for three days; then I'll soon be free of the habit."

And indeed, you soon will be free.

ten

RIGHTS

Recently I was invited to talk to a group of business and civic leaders at a luncheon. The subject was the now-famous Smokers Mystique speech which attempts to explain to nonsmokers why so many otherwise rational people have found themselves entangled in a web of habits, why they persist in smoking though they recognize the risks. To many nonsmokers, it's a "puzzlement," and they often have very little sympathy for smokers. They can't begin to realize the depth and complexity of the habit.

The Smokers Mystique speech generally produces numerous queries. Many are entirely unsympathetic: "Well, if a smoker wants to quit, why doesn't he just stop buying cigarettes? If he had any willpower, he'd just quit!" Some responses are more thoughtful: "Isn't there a drug or hospital treatment to cure the smoker?" After I have tried to explain the extreme difficulties of quitting (and also talked about why the smokEnder method is effective), the discussion will often turn to problem solving, and questions will arise dealing with controls: restrictions, legislation, prohibition.

Here are a few of the most commonly asked questions:

Q: Doesn't the Surgeon General's warning on the side of each
pack and in each ad effectively restrict consumption? If not,
why not?

A: Sorry, but the warning is almost *never* read by smokers. They
certainly don't read it on each pack; it's familiar. The warning
is not seen each time.

Well-meaning nonsmoking friends also point it out to us. The
remark is the same, whether harshly or gently delivered: "Can't
you read?" (There's almost nothing that provokes a more defensive reaction from us smokers.)

There's hardly a smoker who isn't aware of the hazard. The
warning on the pack beats a dead horse.

One practical result of the warning on the package might
have been to give youngsters second thoughts about starting
to smoke. But a recent informal survey among a group of 14-
to-16-year-old high school students indicated two clear reactions among them. A large percentage felt the warning was
crying "Wolf," because, they reasoned, "If the risk was really
so serious, my dad (or my coach, etc.) would have quit, but he
still smokes, so it's probably just some government/industrial
ploy to manipulate us." The point made by a substantial number revealed a certain enchantment with the danger. Kids love
danger and risk.

Q: Whose rights are being violated when a smoker is forbidden
to smoke in public places?

A: One of the favorite arguments of the tobacco industry is that
smoking should not be controlled anywhere because, as its
representatives are fond of saying in their TV interviews, "If
the antismoking people are allowed to limit where you *smoke*,
we'll soon have to deal with bathwater regulators." The implication is that we will be told how hot or cold our bathwater
should be if we permit federal controls of smoking.

An amusing and succinct answer was offered to the tobacco council's representative on the Tom Snyder *Tomorrow* TV show recently by Clara Gouin, founder of GASP (Group Against Smoke Pollution). "It's not that we're against smoking—or against showers. We'd just like to be sure they're both limited to the bathroom."

But what is the Solomon-like solution that is needed to this vexing problem? Here's how I see it. If one smokes, it was his personal choice to start and it remains his personal choice to continue. In the words of some reasonable smokers, "It's *my* life. I'll choose the risks I'll take, and as long as it doesn't hurt anyone, I'll decide when to smoke and when to quit."

Let's explore the other side of the argument—the nonsmoker's. This person is usually not belligerent, but he may be conscious of pollution and trying to avoid unnecessary exposure. Or he may be hypersensitive, even allergic, to smoke, so that his eyes water, his throat tightens, his digestion sours, his head aches. He complains that smokers are fouling his air, violating his rights and making him very uncomfortable.

So the issue becomes "Who should be made uncomfortable in favor of whom?"

Here are a few situations in which smokers and nonsmokers may find themselves locked up with each other. Check what you would believe would be fair:

	SMOKING ALLOWED	NO SMOKING
City buses (short distance)	——	——
Interstate buses (long distance)	——	——
Elevators	——	——
Movie theaters	——	——
Libraries	——	——
Airplanes	——	——
Offices	——	——
Factories	——	——

Grocery stores   —   —
Retail stores   —   —
Elementary schools
   Faculty only—anywhere   —   —
   Faculty only—limited to Faculty Lounge   —   —
Junior high (Middle) schools
   Faculty only—limited to Faculty Lounge   —   —
   Students—limited to smoking room   —   —
   Students—limited to outside building   —   —
Senior high school
   Faculty only—anywhere
           (including classrooms)   —   —
           limited to faculty lounge   —   —
   Students—anywhere
           (including classrooms)   —   —
           limited to smoking room   —   —
Colleges/Universities
   Everyone—anywhere   —   —
           limited to lounges   —   —
School gymnasiums during sports events   —   —
Public sports arenas   —   —
Restaurants   —   —
Subway stations   —   —
Subway cars   —   —
Hospitals   —   —
   Patients' rooms (unless oxygen is being ad-
   ministered)   —   —
   Waiting rooms   —   —
   Visitors   —   —
   Professional staff   —   —
   Administrative staff   —   —
   Maintenance personnel   —   —
Homes of nonsmokers—ashtrays on display   —   —
             no ashtrays visible   —   —

Where do *you* draw the line on legal restrictions? The question of
rights enters. It would be ideal if smokers and nonsmokers could be

segregated in all public areas—but even I would object to forced separation, since "some of my best friends are smokers." However, as you may have discovered when you answered the quiz, there are some natural situations which are logically inopportune. The patient's room in a hospital, for instance.

In a perfect world, there would be no smoking, or drinking, or bad breath, or unattractive and poorly adjusted people. But since the world doesn't work that way, we must establish some rules based upon consideration and good manners. It's surely obvious that we can't legislate morality.

At smokEnders we take the position that smokers have rights and if people want to smoke, that's their business, and if they want to quit, that's our business. We don't believe in hassling smokers. As former smokers, we're not offended by smoke, but feel somewhat sad for smokers. We're sorry for them because they haven't yet learned the pleasure of not—smoking. That may sound condescending, but when you quit smoking the right way, you will very likely feel the same way. In fact, here's a trick we teach in the smokEnder program which you can use: For the next week, observe smokers. Watch them light up and perform the ritual. Really watch them (but don't be obnoxious about it). You'll be amazed how few look as glamorous or masculine or feminine as the ads convey. You'll discover that the majority of smokers look a little chalky, washed out and less than sparkly.* You'll also realize that most aren't even aware they are lighting up or smoking. It's a terrific first step toward changing your attitude about smoking and about your image.

Perhaps the legal line should be drawn in circumstances where people have no choice but to congregate—in schools, offices, hospitals, stores and so on. And since it has been estimated that

---

*This is not imagination. Nicotine, carbon monoxide and the other noxious elements affect the circulation, especially the skin and extremities and soft tissues. A smoker's skin is starved for fresh blood circulation; the eyes have been irritated and are therefore not as clear and bright as a nonsmoker's.

over 30 percent of all fires are caused by cigarette smoking, it would seem practical to limit smoking in areas where there is a present fire hazard. If we carried that to the extreme, and since every stuffed sofa and chair and every mattress is a fire hazard, smoking would be limited even in homes.

Not long ago there was a tragedy in an old, established residential area. A woman of about thirty, the mother of five young children, was recuperating from minor surgery. One night she stayed up later than the rest of the family to watch TV and smoke another cigarette. The house—a solid stone building—was reduced to a shell by dawn. Four children jumped out of windows, but the husband and one boy are both physically and emotionally scarred. She was found in her smoldering easy chair, one more victim of a cigarette fire. Apparently she fell asleep smoking. She was asphyxiated, and then flames did their very thorough job of destroying the house. It was unbelievable—and so unnecessary.

Another example of fire danger is Steve L., who came to one of the first smokEnder meetings. His face was badly scarred. And he smoked.

A routine procedure at smokEnders introductory meetings is to ask, "Why do you want to quit smoking?" Steve's answer is one I'll never forget. He told how he had been smoking in bed several years before. A fire had cost the life of his youngest daughter, the loss of all his possessions and, he said, pointing to his face, "this nightmare of a face." He had gone on smoking.

Even with the grotesqueness of his face, he was an appealing person and very articulate. He described the agony of lighting up each cigarette and the self-hate that accompanied it each time. He talked about his nightmares, about his constant panic about the possibility of having left a lighted cigarette in the house.

Steve joined the program and learned to disconnect all the conditions of smoking that had held him captive. He frequently turns up at meetings in the area to tell his story and encourage others to give quitting the best shot they've got.

In any case, the line on legal restriction of smoking is a difficult one to draw. It affects not only the health of the individual and the comfort of the nonsmoker, but also everyone's safety.

And there's another area to consider. It's been estimated that 30 percent of all auto accidents are directly or indirectly caused by smoking. We've all had the stuck-lip situation, in which we've lit a cigarette, we try to remove it from our lips and it remains stuck and our fingers slip onto the burning end. That's quite a distraction for a driver. There's the whole business of lighting up while driving. Trying to match the business end of the lighter to the cigarette while keeping your eye on speeding traffic is not the simplest trick. Too often we take our eyes away from the road for a split second to make the contact. Or the lighter isn't working, and you start the one-handed match-lighting trick. It's tough enough when you're able to concentrate on that and nothing else, but when your eyes and mind are on the road, it's murder. And suppose the matchbook bursts into flame and drops on your lap, or the cigarette lighter falls on the floor and you start reaching around for it?

How should that be restricted? Forbid drivers to smoke. That's outrageous, I know, but there are some answers to this problem. At the end of the chapter, I'll list some of my suggestions for sane and reasonable approaches.

Q: If smoking is really a serious hazard to the health of the nation, why doesn't the government declare a prohibition and forbid smoking and sale of cigarettes?

A: This is the obvious, reasonable solution—except that it's impractical and has been proved unworkable. Prohibition of liquor certainly demonstrated that it's impossible to legislate morality. In fact, it is a good case study of human nature. We seem to have a mechanism within us that resists being told we *must* do such-and-such; we *must not* do such-and-such. The very act of being told we can't makes us insist we will. The fallacy of the argument is not in the ability of the court to outlaw smoking, the sale of tobacco or being in possession of

it (as with marijuana)—but rather in the assumption that
smokers will simply stop needing and getting their cigarettes.

A smoker *needs* his cigarettes and will go to some lengths to
obtain his dose. Unless and until each smoker alive has freed
himself from the habit, and until the models for our children
(parents, sports figures, doctors, actors and actresses, teachers,
etc.) don't smoke (or at least don't smoke in public)—only then
could a prohibition of some sort be imposed. Even then, there will
be some who smoke and they'll have to be willing to pay a high
price for the privilege. Until then, any sort of prohibition will
invite bootlegging.

What can be done to eliminate this serious health problem
from our society? I believe it must come from society itself,
instead of from the courts. The smokEnder movement is directed
toward "social" change—toward the day when smoking will be
socially unacceptable.

"Nice" people simply won't be caught smoking in public. Ashtrays and smoking in public will be relegated to the same igno-
miny as the spittoon. How will it happen? It's happening now.
More of the men and women who come to smokEnder seminars
say that they're uncomfortably aware that they're the last smoker
in their group: the bridge club, the car pool, the executive committee. Insurance companies are offering reduced rates to nonsmokers. Conventions of medical, dental and insurance professionals don't permit smoking during the sessions—and certainly
no longer place ashtrays on the table routinely. (An amusing aside:
Recently I attended a convention of a state dental society, and
the gift to the ladies was a fine little Wedgwood ashtray. Somebody on the committee hadn't gotten the word!)

There are other examples of the social disapprobation that
smoking now carries. President Kennedy insisted that no member
of his family smoke in public or be photographed smoking. Fashion photographer Lillian Bassman of New York commented recently that style in the haute couture magazines has changed

considerably in regard to smoking. It used to be that all fashion models were posed with a cigarette—often with a long, elegant cigarette holder, sometimes not, but always with a cigarette. Now, she observes, it is rare to find a high-fashion ad showing the model with a cigarette—except, of course, in cigarette ads.

Hostesses aren't putting cigarettes out anymore; in fact, many have even stopped putting out ashtrays. The general attitude seems to be "If someone smokes and needs an ashtray, they will ask for one and I'll provide it. I'm making a statement to my guests: smoking isn't encouraged in this house."

There's an important case, which may well lead to changes in the working environment, protecting working space from the contamination of smoke. In the past, a nonsmoker in a room of smoking employees was expected by common practice to endure the smoke-filled room during working hours. Now that's been changed, since a test case was brought to court against AT&T by a nonsmoking employee, Donna Shimp. Because of serious allergies, Ms. Shimp was not so much offended as affected by smoke. She claimed the smoking environment was injurious to her health and prevented her from working, and that AT&T was required to provide employees with a safe environment. I believe AT&T tried to solve the problem by terminating her, but she took the case to court and won. The judge ordered the company to prohibit smoking in working areas. As I understand it, AT&T was forced to pay lost earnings, rehire her and provide her with non-smoking office space.

Another big step was taken in the direction of making smoking socially unacceptable when the Third World Conference on Smoking and Health, held in New York City in 1975 at the Waldorf Astoria, accepted two resolutions by Dr. Jerome Jaffe of New York's Columbia Presbyterian Medical Center:

    1. that nicotine is addictive and should be viewed as socially detrimental;

    2. that smoking be classified as a condition, rather than simply a habit.

His recommendation of the term "compulsive smoking syndrome" was approved by the conference. These two statements placed smoking in a new category: it is an addiction, and addiction is socially unacceptable. Doctors now have a classification that implies a complex syndrome, and I hope they will deal with it in a more realistic fashion. Instead of giving a command to stop smoking, they will come to prescribe treatment by experts in the field.

Here are some proposals to change the public's attitude about the social acceptability of smoking:

While faculty lounges in schools are a social smoking place, students will say, "Why is it okay for my teachers to smoke and not okay for me? If smoking is harmful, isn't it harmful for them too?" Either it should be banned in schools altogether, or a special smoking room should be provided for smokers in school. This would also make the fire chief much happier.

Newspapers: Obituary columns should state whether the deceased was a smoker or not and whether the cause of death was cancer or the cause of a fire was by cigarette.

Fire departments should record and announce the number and percentage of fires caused by cigarette smoking and provide newspapers with the facts. Then a strong smoker-education program should be initiated to make smokers aware of the risk and reduce the loss of lives and property caused by smoking.

As proposed by the World Conference on Smoking and Health, not-smoking should be a condition of acceptance into medical and dental schools and into teacher-education programs.

Hospitals: Restrictions should be imposed requiring the professional staff to refrain from smoking anywhere in public. The health professionals have the greatest responsibility for prevention of disease and saving lives. Their example is most effective. In fact, it has been said that a doctor doesn't just risk his own life —he affects the attitude of all who see him smoke.

The Media: Fashion and sport magazines should avoid using scenes with models who are smoking; TV should self-enforce smoking standards. Smoking simply shouldn't be shown on TV. This goes for movies as well. An interesting thrust could be made by movie directors and producers if they were to portray the bad guy as a smoker and the good guy as the one who never smokes. It would be just like the old Westerns. We always knew who the villain was—the guy in the black hat! Theatrical directors could make a subtle statement about the acceptability of smoking by writing the habit out of the script wherever it is used to demonstrate a character's sophistication or cool.

What About an Etiquette of Smoking?

The essence of the problem isn't rights, it's common courtesy. Smokers aren't willfully trying to offend nonsmokers. We're just thoughtless because we haven't ever been taught smoking manners. The only effort has been to teach smokers to ask, "Do you mind if I smoke?"—but we smokers have always perceived the question as rhetorical. When I smoked, if someone were to answer, "Yes, I mind," I would have been stunned. I hadn't really asked his permission; I was just going through an accepted ritual. What right had he to suggest I shouldn't smoke?

Well, we've come a long way, baby. The shoe is on the other foot. There are now more nonsmokers in this country than smokers, and the silent majority is beginning to be less silent. . . .

Before we have a bloody war between smokers and nonsmokers —with ex-smokers caught in the middle—let's strike for a compromise. Here's a suggestion:

The tobacco industry, which now spends about $350,000,000 annually on advertising, should take some responsibility for promoting smoking etiquette. Perhaps the industry could allocate 10 percent of its budget for goodwill advertising and provide a booklet of good smoking manners. Some of these good manners might even spill over into general behavior.

What incentive would the cigarette manufacturers have to

invest this kind of money? Certainly, they would improve their image. Changing bad manners of smokers to meet standards acceptable to the nonsmoking faction would reduce the irritation quotient considerably. Booklets on smoking manners would be only one step in their goodwill project. If our government ever clamps down on print advertising of cigarettes, as it has done with TV and radio, as many of the European countries have done, beautiful, high-powered ads could present the niceties of smoking somewhat as follows:

If you choose to smoke, show consideration for those who choose not to smoke in this way:

Don't place a burning cigarette on a tabletop or any other piece of furniture, especially if you don't own the furniture.

Do not place a lighted cigarette on a toilet-tank top, toilet-paper holder, sink, washroom shelf or other horizontal surface in a public or private washroom; it leaves a permanent stain.

It isn't good form to stomp out a cigarette on a carpet or a wooden floor. Find an ashtray, or flush it down the toilet if necessary.

Don't stomp it out on someone's lawn or toss it into a garden. People feel as protective about their outdoor property as about their indoor living quarters and have to pick up your butts after you leave.

When you are a guest in someone's home or office and no ashtrays are in evidence, it generally means the host prefers that you not smoke. It may be his or her way of saying, "Please don't smoke in this room." However, most people are taught to be gracious, so if you must smoke, ask for an ashtray. More often than not, you may be given one.

If your hosts ask you to refrain from smoking while in their company, it isn't polite to light up anyhow. If your need to smoke is so great that you can't wait, excuse yourself for a moment, walk to an outside area, take a quick smoke to relieve your craving and return to the company relaxed.

At meals, please don't light up while others are still eating. It is really very inconsiderate of nonsmokers, whose sense of taste allows them to enjoy the nuances of flavor; the pungent odor of smoke ruins delicate flavors. This is particularly important if you're a guest at a special meal: it is clearly understood by all that smoking is not permitted between courses, even if the meal continues for several hours, as is usually the case.

More personally, when you expect to be physically close to someone—co-workers, fellow students, girl or boy friend or spouse —or in special situations such as acting a love scene in a play, or explaining something that requires close contact, or above all in the dentist's chair, have mercy on the other fellow and use a good mouthwash beforehand. Ordinary occasional bad breath is bad enough, but the constant foul odor that develops in a smoker's mouth is repulsive to others. When you impose it on others by your closeness, very few people have the nerve to tell you you're offending them. "Even your best friends won't tell you" is a fact of life. If you're wondering why people don't get too close to you, or they hold their hands near their faces while they talk to you, you'll notice the extent of your thoughtlessness. (After you stop smoking, you'll be horrified to realize that you once offended as much as you're offended now.)

It's also important that you take very good care of your clothes and person to get rid of smoke odor. Your clothes hold the odor of smoking that you may not smell.

Both mouth and body odors should be carefully considered before you engage in sex, unless your partner is a smoker too. Make every effort to defume yourself. But don't just try to cover up the odors with breath fresheners and perfume. Instead, eat apples to freshen your breath, and take a long bath. Happily, when you stop smoking, you can stop worrying about body, clothes and breath odor, but until then be considerate of your partner's pleasure.

The smoker's code of etiquette also includes close-quarter situations such as elevators. It is poor form, as well as against the law in New York, to enter an elevator with a lighted cigarette. It is worse to light up after entering.

Cars: If you ride with nonsmokers, avoid smoking during the trip, since the smoke is particularly noxious when it stagnates in the interior of a car.

On long trips, when your need to smoke becomes oppressive, you might ask the driver to stop at the next rest stop for a few moments. If you're embarrassed to tell him you just want to smoke, you might imply you need a bathroom stop.

Public rest rooms: Generally, these are small and poorly ventilated, so good manners will rule out smoking while you are attending to your personal needs; certainly you won't want to loiter in that environment just to smoke. This is particularly important in schools, where nonsmoking classmates have to use the same washroom.

Small offices, study cubicles, dorm rooms: The rule is very much the same as for private homes and offices: if nonsmokers are present and/or if no ashtrays are visible, don't smoke. Leave the room if necessary. Small rooms haven't enough air space to dilute the smoke, carbon monoxide and other gases that a cigarette generates. Not only do you risk offending your friends, but you run a good chance of making them crabby and cranky. They react without realizing it, even if they aren't concerned about breathing polluted air or standing up for their "rights"—because carbon monoxide causes a good deal of physical discomfort. In large doses, under certain conditions, it causes death. Although you aren't killing your friends with your cigarettes, you're giving them a low-level dose of poisonous gas which affects their nervous systems.

When assigning dorm rooms to students, many schools now ask if you smoke or not, in order to slot smokers together. Too many arguments start when the smoker becomes irritated because the nonsmoker asks him not to smell up the room. You can imagine the rest.

As a new smoker you must keep in mind that blowing smoke in someone's face is very impolite. Try to imagine that the smoke is black instead of white, and that it leaves a sooty residue on everything it touches, and that the residue can be seen on faces, tablecloths, hair, windows, typewriters, food. And then try to imagine that vapors from your lungs and bacteria from your mouth get mixed with the smoke and are visible as you exhale. Imagine your embarrassment if the person with whom you are having lunch were to end up with a moist, black, sooty film covering his face, hair, lunch, books and clothes.

That's exactly what you're doing, except that it's not visible. In addition, you would very likely cause his eyes to water and his nose and throat to feel irritated because he isn't used to smoke. So, needless to say, good manners require that you aim your smoke in a different direction.

Then there's the matter of allowing your cigarette to slowly smolder in an ashtray because you're busy or have forgotten to stub it out. This forces a different kind of imposition upon others. Side-stream smoke is much more pungent and harmful to non-smokers than smoke which has at least been filtered through your lungs, especially when it comes from a butt whose filter is burning. Etiquette requires that you not leave your cigarette smoldering in an ashtray too long; and when you stub it out, extinguish it completely.

To be really considerate, douse your butts with water and empty your ashtrays yourself, instead of expecting others to clean up after you. Too often smoldering butts are tossed into the wastebasket when the ashtrays are emptied. It is more than courtesy to make sure your butts are "dead": it can be a matter of life and death.

There are many more situations that new and old smokers should learn to consider so that smokers and nonsmokers can coexist in reasonable harmony.

eleven

WHAT DO YOU SAY TO SOMEONE YOU LOVE WHO SMOKES?

Trying to help someone protect himself from disease by suggesting he quit smoking can boomerang. The scenario is not uncommon. Here are some typical scenes.

The Lindquists have been married for about 25 years. It has been a good marriage—they've grown together and raised fine children. Arthur manages the small plumbing firm his father started. He is involved in the Lions Club, with Sight Saving as his pet project. He's moved up from Tail Twister to President and has a reputation for being a great sport.

Recently, Art developed a morning cough. He gags and coughs until he turns purple. Clara was suspicious that smoking aggravates his cough and decided to speak to him about it.

"Arthur, why don't you stop smoking for a while, so you can recover from that cough?" she suggested casually one morning.

He was defensive. "That cough has nothing to do with my smoking. It's just the dampness at the shop. I've ordered a new ceiling heater which should take care of it."

The cough got worse, and Clara began worrying about it. She suggested Art see a doctor. He was adamant. "Nothing is wrong with me. I'm fit as a fiddle. Lots of people cough—nothing to be alarmed about," he said impatiently.

His attitude was uncharacteristic, and the more she observed Art, the more she worried and the more certain she was that smoking was to blame. One day she bought a filter kit at the drugstore. The counter display said it could help the user to quit smoking. So she sprang it on Art at suppertime.

He almost growled at her as he threw it into the wastebasket. "Who said I wanted to quit smoking?" he asked. "If I want to quit, I will. I can quit anytime I want to," he said.

Lately Clara has become sarcastic about Art's cough and his smoking. Frustrated, she resorts to comments like "Oh, yes, we know when Art's home. His cough can be heard clear to Columbus. But he doesn't care!" Or, "Well, Art's going to smoke himself to death and I'll be a rich widow." Or, "He just doesn't have the willpower, and he isn't man enough to admit it and go for help."

A rift has developed between them. Clara doesn't understand how it happened—and Art is relieved when Clara isn't around to nag him about his smoking. Lately he has stopped at the bar for longer and longer before coming home after work. It's a rotten impasse.

Here is another illustration:

Jeannie Richardson, an attractive sophomore at Cornell, has been a regular smoker for about four years—since she started senior high school.

Her father smokes. Her mother never did. Her older brother, a medical student and varsity tennis star, quit smoking in high school because of his tennis. Jeannie is strong-willed and determined to take her place in the business world. She doesn't like to be told what to do or to take second place in anything.

Jeannie's mother often expresses disappointment that Jeannie smokes. "When I was a young girl," she says, "it was considered unladylike for young ladies to smoke." To which Jeannie quickly responds, "Those days are gone forever, Mother. We've come a long way, baby," as she dramatically and ceremoniously lights up to prove her point. Or, under friendlier circumstances, Jeannie will say, "But, Mother, all the girls smoke now. It's not what it used to be. And it helps so much when I'm studying and am under pressure—or when I'm bored."

When Jeannie's father is bothered to see her smoke (for reasons he can't seem to articulate), Jeannie is quick to remind him that he smokes, so it can't be so bad or he'd quit.

Once he tried to make a bet with her to see if they'd both quit together, but Jeannie refused. "You should be able to quit by yourself, Dad, because you've smoked a longer time than I. I enjoy smoking and want to go on until I'm closer to the time when it might hurt me. Then I'll quit."

When her father asked how she'd be smart enough to know in advance when it would be harmful, she said, "Well, I won't quite know in *advance*, but the minute the doctor tells me to quit, I'll quit."

Jeannie's father was defenseless. That was the reasoning he'd been using for the past twenty years. Lately he's worried; His doctor has told him to stop smoking because his breathing isn't what it should be for a man his age. There is a possibility of emphysema, the doctor has said. He has tried, secretly, to quit. But the more he worries about his health, the more he seems to want to smoke.

How can he tell Jeannie that it doesn't quite work the way she thinks it will? That once you're told, "You must stop smoking" not only might it be too late, but it becomes unbearably difficult?

So what do you tell people you love who smoke? Obviously there are different answers depending on whether you want to protect children, whether you're a smoker yourself, whom you want to help.

First the no's:

1. Don't command them to stop smoking. Even if they're young, it's risky and often not successful. You're forcing them into opposition, forcing them to assert themselves.

2. Don't nag or harass. "Do you have to smoke another cigarette? You just put one out!" is perhaps the most common and

most irritating comment to a smoker. Probably most used by nonsmoking parents to their children, it compels them to reinforce their position by thinking up new reasons why they need that next cigarette. You produce the same result by hiding their packs or yanking a cigarette from their hands. And don't think you're not nagging if you constantly clean up ashtrays after them. Even if you say you hate the smell of stale smoke and ash, and you probably do, you're really making the statement that you're a martyr to their smoking habit and want to make them uncomfortable. Remember what we said about martyrdom earlier on? It doesn't work.

3.Don't intimidate or demean by implying lack of character or willpower. Most smokers are aware that they shouldn't smoke; it's unfair, unkind and unproductive to bruise their egos. Don't criticize, and don't put up No Smoking signs, or you'll end up very lonely.

So what can you do to help someone come to terms with the smoking habit? Before I make some constructive suggestions, I'll tell you about the two events that affected me most in my struggle.

For years my family waged direct and open warfare on my smoking habit. It was too often the topic of conversation. And the more they'd hide my cigarettes, the more reinforced the habit became. Soon the very subject of smoking became an unpleasant one in our house. I would become defensive, my husband would become angry and the children felt helpless. Their helplessness and anguish proved to be a turning point in my attitude toward quitting.

One morning, our son Jim, then about 11 years old, came down for breakfast looking very pale and scared. I asked what was the matter, because he was generally a lively, happy boy.

"Oh, Mother," he said, "I had a nightmare. It was awful. I don't even want to think about it anymore, but I can't get it out of my mind."

"Tell me about it, Jim, and maybe it'll help to get it into the sunlight," I suggested.

"I dreamt we were at a place where there was a big wire fence, like the one around Grumman Aircraft on Long Island that we pass on the way to East Marion. It was taller than a person and seemed to be endless. Growing on this fence was a vine with big, shiny leaves. The vine was all over the fence as far as I could see. And on top of each section of fence there were signs. Big red signs, with neon lights blinking on and off."

He was showing terror even as he spoke, reliving his dream. He was trembling and on the brink of tears. But he went on. "The signs said, 'Warning. Do not touch these vines. Deadly poisonous upon contact.' "

He couldn't seem to bring himself to finish. So I waited a moment and then tried to help him.

"And did you see yourself touching them, somehow, Jim, and that's what terrified you?" I asked.

He started to cry, and sobbing, said, "No, Mom, it was you! You had a basket, and you were picking the leaves and singing and saying how beautiful they were. When I tried to pull you away, and tried to show you the signs and begged you to stop picking the leaves, you just smiled and said, 'Silly little boy, they won't hurt me—and they're so beautiful.' " Now he was unable to continue.

And now I was shaken, too.

And then he said one more thing, which hit home.

"I don't want you to die, Mom . . . I'm scared. And—and"—his voice and eyes lowered—"you didn't seem to care how I felt."

I asked him if he had any idea what the dream meant, but at 11 one is not very sophisticated at dream interpretation. He said he didn't know, but it was horrible and he was scared.

I hugged him and assured him it was only a dream and that he shouldn't worry.

But I had felt the impact of his dream. It had given me a clear glimpse of the deep hurt I was causing my family by my cavalier attitude toward potential illness and premature death.

To have an insight is a powerful experience. Although it's rare to really see inside a situation, into yourself or into your behavior, it can, when it happens, unleash a tremendously strong, though latent, motivation.

Jim's dream unleashed in me a great desire to quit, but I still had the obstacle of knowing how. Because I had been so unsuccessful in the past, I was unable to respond immediately to my heightened motivation. That's when the next event took place. Jon, in his wisdom, decided it was time to stop the talk and find a way to do something about the problem. So he said, "Jackie, I know you have tried to quit very sincerely in the past, and I realize now that the smoking habit is more complicated than I thought. I understand that before you're able to quit smoking you have a problem to solve. But I have a problem too as a result. My problem is that I have the responsibility to protect my family, and especially our children. It would be unforgivable if I didn't do everything in my power to see that our children have their mother for as long as they need her. And I anticipate the day when smoking will finally cut you down. What shall I tell our children as we stand at the graveside and they look up at me and say, 'But Daddy, why did you let Mommy smoke?' "

He paused. "If you can tell me what to say, I won't bother you again about your smoking."

Jon wasn't cornering me just to show how clever or superior he was; he had a plan.

So when I wailed, "Oh, Jon—I've tried so hard to quit, but I can't. I'm weak. I'm stupid. I'm rotten to do this to you all. But I *can't* quit smoking," he had an answer.

"Yes, I know the problem," he said, "and I've done something about it. I have told the children the only way we could help Mother work out her problem was to give her the opportunity to really study the whole business of smoking and quitting. To give her time to research and work on the problem thoroughly, we would have to help with her daily chores like the laundry, grocery shopping and the cooking and cleaning.

"I asked them if they'd be willing to pitch in, if you'd be willing to give it a try," he added, "and they were enthusiastic."

This was an offer I couldn't refuse, because it was made in such an understanding way. And it was a positive suggestion, not an intimidating command.

The rest of the story is history. I did my research. The family did the chores. I worked out a method with which I could succeed and which left me with a feeling of personal freedom and enjoyment of not-smoking. And here I am, nine years later, writing a book to try and pass on what I've learned.

Here are my suggestions for helping others effectively:

What do you tell a youngster you love who smokes? Obviously, the problem is touchy. Young people are very much involved with the development of their own money and their images of themselves. One reason they may have begun to smoke was to challenge authority; for many of us smokers it was a rite of growing up. So you can explain that smoking is dangerous, but that may only make it more attractive: high-risk, glamorous, grown-up.

A spontaneous discussion can work, especially if it takes place with a slightly older peer who may have quit smoking because "it was kid stuff!" But obviously you can't count on that.

A wry aside came from my son Peter, aged 15, who wrote from school about being an overnight guest of a friend's. His young hostess, who smoked herself, was very much worried about her father's heavy smoking. "I spoke to one of her friends who says that smoking is uncool past about 8th grade, and she feels there's nothing wrong with not smoking."

I had to read it again: "Smoking is uncool past the 8th grade." If that's where it's at with the young generation, I'm hopeful. But it's not always that easy. I've worked with students 13 years old who had smoked for five years and were unable to quit without a program. They were as hooked as adults who had smoked for thirty years. Some of them wanted to quit and did.

If the "kid stuff" doesn't work directly, you will have to find a more subtle lure. "I'll have confidence that you can control your behavior and let you go hiking in Europe (or whatever the project is) if you can demonstrate that you're mature enough to stop smoking."

Make a contract with the young person. Discuss your feelings with him (or her); explain your realistic concern about giving him the best chance to grow up healthy. Promise that if he gives up smoking now and saves all his cigarette money, you'll match it each month until his twenty-second birthday. (The statistics indicate that people rarely start smoking after 22.) Spend an evening calculating how much money he would accumulate over the years —with compound interest and rising tobacco costs and taxes factored in. Think aloud about what he could buy with that money. It will give him a first concrete idea of how much money might well "go up in smoke." It will also bring you both closer. Children appreciate nothing more than time their parents devote to them.

But what if you smoke yourself? How can you convince children that they'd be better off without smoking? The best way, of course, is to try, at least, to stop. That's what Jeannie's father should have done, especially when he apparently realized that his health was being affected.

I hope, by the time you have read this far, you will have found another way of approaching the subject as well. Otherwise, there's only one real alternative and that is to level with your youngsters. "Do as I say, not as I do" is not an easy way to convince anybody, especially your own children. Young people have a strict sense of what's fair. You'll have to explain that you started to smoke long before it was known to be so hazardous and that now you find you're unable to quit because cigarettes are addictive and you're hooked. That's why you want them to stop before it's too late. Assure them that you'll try again and that it will be easier for you if they don't smoke. A good way to help them is to make them help you.

Much of what we've said holds true when it isn't your children, but a spouse or a dear friend who must or should quit smoking and who needs help. If you are smoking too, but perhaps less, or you aren't feeling any ill effects yet, the best way is still to make a pact—at least, a joint effort.

You might be tempted to say, "Well, I don't smoke that much, only a couple of cigarettes a day, and I don't inhale." In that case, of course, it shouldn't be very hard for you to give up those few cigarettes. It makes the struggle so much easier when there is loving cooperation; when there are no cigarettes around to provide temptation; when there isn't any smell to serve as a reminder of past "enjoyment."

And as you have seen from my own example, the greatest help is manifest understanding and encouragement. You can sympathize with the hardship even if you've never smoked yourself. Don't criticize the other person's crankiness and irritability, which you should recognize as withdrawal symptoms. Say instead, "I can't quite imagine what it's like, but I respect you for trying. I believe in you."

But if the smoker cannot be persuaded to make an attempt at quitting, all you can really say is "I realize smoking must be a very complex and deeply personal thing. I've come to recognize that it is your problem. I can't force you to quit, and I can't quit for you. I can only tell you that I love you and believe in you and that I wish you wouldn't smoke because I'm looking forward to having many happy, healthy years with you. But it's your life, and I know you'll do the right thing when you're ready."

twelve

HUNCHES ABOUT WHY PEOPLE SMOKE; WHETHER SMOKERS ARE DIFFERENT; WHY PEOPLE GO ON SMOKING

One of our more delightful smokEnder graduates is Chandler Sterling, an Episcopal bishop. He puzzled over the phenomenon of his smoking, his previous failures and his reasons for starting to smoke in the first place. He had a lot to say about the fact that he knows that smoking contradicted his deeply felt belief that the body is the temple of the soul.

Bishop Sterling is an unusual man, with wide-ranging interests; a man of the world as well as of the spirit; and he has a keen sense of humor. He has written a book about hockey. He's a sensitive person who is deeply concerned with the individual's day-to-day response to life. He told me one day about a conclusion he'd come to after a great deal of thought.

He thinks that a lot of us start smoking because it's a form of "gleeful sinning."

That is rather profound in a simple way. And I can't disagree with him. It could be one of the reasons why people start. A lot of reasons have been well and often quoted. But I'm not really trying to find the reasons why people start or continue to smoke. I'm convinced that people smoke because they don't know how to quit, that they haven't been properly prepared. I have tried to find why some of us, many of whom tried when they were young, did *not* take it up. My files are full of interviews with people who do not smoke, never have smoked. Why didn't they pursue it after that first necessary try? Why didn't they subject themselves to the same demanding learning process we did: the dizziness, the gagging and coughing, the awkwardness of the whole ritual, the embarrassment when we tried it out in front of others and they laughed, the burning throat and eyes?

Why did some people, like my husband, try a cigarette now and then and then decide consciously that it was not for them? Here are some insights I am led to consider.

One large group felt it didn't do anything for them and even wondered why others put themselves to the cost and trouble. Another group felt it was kind of dirty and expensive, and that their parents didn't approve. Another group tried it and gave it up because of the physical discomfort. Another, rather unusual, group confessed they had tried and tried to take it up because they felt inferior in the army and in college or business as nonsmokers. This group reported unusual difficulties in starting to smoke and never achieved their objective. One friend in Providence, Rhode Island, a successful businessman and scholar, the father of four daughters, confessed a particular conscious embarrassment when he was younger because he didn't feel like one of the guys.

He's one of the guys now. Recently he mentioned to me how delighted he was that he finally feels in the majority and doesn't have to apologize for not smoking. Here's a man who very much wanted to smoke but was somehow repelled from the practice.

I have some hunches about the difference between those of us who took up smoking and those who didn't. There are factors I suspect must come into play, and one of them is youngsters' feelings about themselves. For instance, if they were generally popular, together, talented or accomplished in a particular field such as drama, music, sports, scholastics; if they felt good about themselves; the chances were *somewhat* less that they would start to smoke. It's still true. And that's very reasonable. And understandable. Except it doesn't hold up across the board. There are a large number of people who were very unhappy with themselves as teens, had a poor regard for themselves, but didn't start smoking.

One of my hunches has to do with body chemistry. I call it the "salt-lick" theory. You remember learning that deer need salt and search for "salt licks," such as the lichen that is on the shady side of the tree, around the moss. They know by instinct that they need salt. And they look for it. Nature provides them with a way of replacing a missing element. It's not a learned hunger; it satisfies the need. These deer didn't develop a taste for salty things by munching on potato chips and peanuts during childhood.

Translate that to smokers, and you may suspect that some people smoke to make up a lack of something in their chemistry. The hunch seems to hold up in practice. An important section of the smokEnder program deals with fatigue and lack of energy and the use of cigarette smoking to elevate the blood sugar. Many smokEnder graduates value that self-knowledge and say it helped them to kick the habit, to live at a fairly high energy level without cigarettes. It would be an interesting experiment to measure the blood-sugar level of teen-agers, and perhaps their thyroid activity, and then, when they were about 25, to see which ones were confirmed smokers. My hunch tells me that those with below-average blood sugar and/or thyroid activity would be found among the smokers. Nicotine elevates the blood-sugar level, and each cigarette is a boost—a boost with a real kicker for the beginning smoker especially. The boost diminishes over the years and eventually is only a flicker. By then it's become a different problem.

On the other hand, it must be true that there are people who react badly to the chemicals in cigarettes, who have a reaction similar to hay fever, perhaps even stronger.

Also, there must be something to be learned about how people perceive taste—in this case, the taste of cigarettes. Discounting the fact that most ads importune us to believe that we smoke for the taste, that the taste is good, I don't believe cigarettes taste good to most smokers.

If, for beginners, the taste of the first few cigarettes is perceived as vile and bitter, it could account for their not being tempted to take up smoking. It must be admitted, however, that most of us who yielded to the lure, who overcame all the difficulty, would admit that the first cigarette didn't taste so wonderful. Just as those first cups of coffee were disappointing. But to perceive a taste as vile is far from finding it a disappointment.

My hunch picked up some steam with the discovery that if monosodium glutamate is taken during the day it can cause cigarettes to taste bitter in the evening. I've been unable to track the source of that finding, but in a random testing among friends, it appears to hold up.

So here's another surprise trick to help you observe your smoking and perhaps change some conditions. Use some MSG on your food at lunchtime and you'll cut down on your evening smoking. Try it; but be certain you don't feel obliged to stuff food into your mouth that night instead of those bitter-tasting cigarettes, or you'll have another problem.

If you're the sort of smoker who could simply throw his cigarettes away if he had enough reason, this might do the trick for you. Many smokers have quit because cigarettes didn't taste good anymore, and some people report that cigarettes suddenly started tasting awful. Here's the hunch. Could it be that something in their body chemistry has changed enough to affect their taste? This is supported by the reaction that many pregnant women have to cigarettes and coffee.

Ah, one could become philosophical, dig deeply into taste, as art students think about color. What is green? Do you see the same thing I see when I see green? Can you describe green to me? What is taste? When you taste something sweet, is it the same thing I call sweet?

These are some things I think bear looking at if we're going to find out why we smoke. The undertaking is not very scientific, but it may help us to think about the satisfactions and answered needs. If we can lay our finger on some of the causes of our smoking, we may be able to find less dangerous and costly alternatives.

It is the need to *feel good* that I think may be a central point in trying to manage the smoking problem. Many of us are often not quite up to par. We want to get things done but we don't quite have the pep. Our energy levels may fall below what it takes to keep abreast of our more energetic colleagues. It's a natural phenomenon: the energy level drops from time to time during each day until the body manufactures more blood sugar to keep up with demand.

When we're little, we take naps. As children, we're put to bed at an early hour. When we become teens, we're more or less on our own schedule. Does it seem farfetched to imagine that the incidence of "tiredness" and peplessness which usually occurs first during our teen years is due to insufficient sleep, as well as other natural changes which occur during adolescence? Could it be that one of the reasons kids take to cigarettes so young is that smoking gives them a physical as well as an emotional boost?

Supporting this hunch is another intriguing guess. Studies have demonstrated that the chance of youngsters' smoking is less if their parents don't smoke. The implication has usually been that example is the prime motivator. "If your parents smoke, the chances are that you will smoke because you see them doing it and it's an accepted behavior" is a commonly accepted theory of the researchers.

I suspect the cause is partly genetic. If both parents smoke, perhaps both parents have the same lack in their body chemistry, and their offspring may have inherited that lack.

Carrying this idea a bit further and considering other areas of excessive (compulsive) behavior, it has been established by research into alcoholism that the offspring of alcoholics are more likely to become alcoholic. This would seem to point in the direction of my hunch even more clearly than the cigarette example: it's much easier to see the abusive effects of alcoholic excess than of smoking. So, one might reason, if a youngster saw his family wrecked and his father/mother deteriorate as a result of drinking, he would avoid that trap. That's not the kind of acceptable example a son or daughter might mimic. And yet alcoholism is said to be handed down.

My theory that some of us need our salt lick still holds even with these examples considered. What is missing that drives a person to hunger for tobacco, alcohol or sweets? The hunch carries over into the tendency to obesity. It too appears to be "inherited," according to current theories, of which the most popular is that fat mothers cook and serve the same fattening foods and serve them in the same fattening quantities they eat. So we become fat because of our eating habits, it is said—habits we "inherited" from thoughtless mothers. Poor mothers: they're blamed for so much.

I submit that we cravers, whether we crave cigarettes, whiskey or candy, have something in common. We frequently feel "lousy" and go in search of sugar or other carbohydrates. Each of these culprits either has a high carbohydrate content or causes a swift elevation of the blood sugar.

Another hunch that has pressed itself on my consciousness since I began my original inquiry is becoming less foolish each year. That was my suspicion that there was a relationship between the peculiar acidy feeling I sometimes had and the amount of smoking I did. I recall vividly the feeling I almost always had when I'd settle down for a long trip by car or bus. I would characterize it as acid indigestion or heartburn, but I knew it wasn't. (I was an old pro at both these feelings, having endured them to a considerable degree during my four pregnancies.) It seems to me that it was a sense of a low-level acidity. Now, as I write this and try to describe it to you, I find I can reconstruct the feeling by thinking about biting into a lemon. My salivary glands start pumping, but more significantly, something in that area which I visualize as above my stomach and below my diaphragm gets queasy or sour. Nevertheless, it was important enough for me to recognize that I reached for a cigarette to quell that feeling. And sure enough, it changed the feeling for a while.

And then I observed that I had that same feeling in some other situations—not necessarily related situations, but generally stressful. The more the feeling persisted, the more I smoked.

Having observed this condition during my close observation of my own smoking patterns, I concluded that it might be useful to try a simple antacid medication to see if it would lessen the number of cigarettes I smoked. It did. When I wrote my own program for stopping smoking, it included a package of Tums. When the sensation of "watery acid" inside me occurred, I popped a Tum instead of a cigarette. I don't understand why, but it worked.

Now, after years of observing other smokers and their high-smoking periods, it seems to me there's a relationship between those of us who produce considerable acid under stress (or because of stress) and those of us who become smokers. It would be terrific to be able to say, "People who have taken up smoking have a higher acid level (produced more acid) than people who don't take up smoking. And the more acid in the system, the more cigarettes are consumed." If this is a fact, and I have a strong hunch it is, then we can do a lot to prevent smokers from starting and aid those who have already started.

Youngsters' acid balance could be quite easily stabilized. In fact, another of my hunches is that youngsters who continue to drink quantities of milk regularly are less likely to start smoking than those who have given up drinking milk at an early age. Milk is alkaline. The lime (calcium) in it can counterbalance the acid in one's system.

Recently, Dr. Stanley Schachter of Columbia University, whom I have already quoted, indicated that tests reveal a high acid content in urine as a result of anxiety and stress. He discovered that smokers who were given mild acids in large doses smoked more over a period of days than comparable smokers who took bicarbonates to make their urine more alkaline. His tests also show that bicarbonates reduce smoking under stress.

Here's what you can do to benefit from this possible relationship:

1. Don't drink orange juice first thing in the morning on an empty stomach. Put something solid into your stomach before your morning juice.

2. Reach for an antacid tablet instead of a cigarette when you feel acidy.

3. Reduce the amount of coffee you drink, which is highly acid. Switch to bouillon from time to time.

4. Drink milk, especially before bedtime and when your "nerves" seem to be taut. This is not just an old wives' remedy; milk is really an "acid balancer."

Another hunch. We have a real need for breathing satisfaction. Think about it. We take breathing for granted, yet it isn't a wholly involuntary action, like the heartbeat. We control our breathing. It's true that we can't hold our breath for too long, but we can regulate how often and how shallowly or deeply we breathe. My hunch is that smokers, taking those regular and deep drags on cigarettes, satisfy a need to breathe deeply. Or indulge themselves in a satisfying feeling.

Smokers who quit cold turkey, and I had observed this about myself when I quit cold turkey, complain of light-headedness. I have watched them sigh deeply, and frequently. They were hyperventilating, as I had done so often. We needed to "feel" ourselves breathing, I think. Deep breathing is essential to well-being.

Here's what you can do to deal with that particular problem before you quit, and be prepared to deal with it after you quit:

1. Learn to breathe deeply without a cigarette. Before you quit, taking long, deep breaths may cause a coughing fit, but it will pass, and you'll experience a similar sense of satisfaction to the one you got from drawing on your cigarette. Next time, before you reach for a cigarette, take one of those long, deep breaths—mouth closed—right down to your toes. Hold it for a

moment or two and then exhale slowly through your mouth.

2. After you quit, whenever the desire for a cigarette hits you, stop what you're doing and take a slow deep breath. In through the nose, out through the mouth. It's like smoking, only better. You don't cough.

3. Don't sigh, and don't overbreathe. It causes light-headedness. It's a form of anesthesia (I used it for natural childbirth).

One last hunch. I think there must be a relationship between a reduction in the amount we breathe after we stop smoking and a slowing down of our metabolism. It may account for why some people gain weight. Oxygen fans the flames of the fire that burns up calories. If the flame burns slowly, calories are not consumed as rapidly. Perhaps when we smoke, the breathing that is involved fans the flames and causes our metabolic furnace to burn more vigorously. If this is the case, it's another reason to take conscious good, long, satisfying deep breaths regularly. But be careful: take only two or three at a time, or you may fade out for a moment.

There are only hunches; they're not meant to pose as scientific wisdom. It may even be that they have merit but for the wrong reasons. But this much I know: I used them to help walk away from cigarettes. I don't smoke anymore. Think about using them. They can't do any harm, and at the least, they should be able to help you cut down. Then, when you're ready to quit, you'll be in gear to do it with grace and style.

thirteen

WHAT CAN MAKE YOU QUIT?

The Stopping-and-Starting Syndrome

"It's easy to quit smoking. I've done it thousands of times," Mark Twain said, and you've probably heard that quote a thousand times. Another you may not have heard before comes from the British magazine *Punch*. When the tobacco tax had once again been raised on Budget Day, *Punch* predicted, "All the people who gave up smoking last year will do so again this year."

Both quotes make the point very clearly.

Whether you're a "passive" quitter who vows, "I'll stop tomorrow" but never skips a cigarette or an active quitter like me— we've all given up smoking from time to time for various reasons. Sometimes we succeed for a few days, a few weeks, even months at a time, and then go back. We're start-and-stop quitters.

In the same category belong the quitting "due to circumstances beyond my control" types. Classic example: when we're really sick, perhaps in an oxygen tent after pneumonia or a heart attack, we can't and don't smoke, sometimes long enough to believe that we've licked the habit. After returning home, when we feel better, the first chance we get puts us right back on the regular pattern.

Why can't we stay away from cigarettes? One accusation is that we smokers have a death wish. That's nonsense. I assure you that even through all the years I smoked, I had a feisty love of life and everything about it. In any case, as we've read, all the recent studies show that most smokers would like to quit if they only knew how. There's no death wish there.

Then we're told we go back to smoking because we're neurotic. I don't believe that either. As I've pointed out before, I believe that we are neurotic because we smoke. Another explanation of our failures, one we begin to believe ourselves, is that we suffer from a peculiar lack of willpower. As start-and-stop quitters we learn to accept failure. The more often we go back to smoking, the more we lose confidence. Slowly the acceptance of that failure spills over into other aspects of our life, just as success does. We quit quitting—it's too humiliating.

Mark Twain didn't have to tell us *why* he quit a thousand times. It doesn't really matter. All smokers know all the reasons why they should quit. They try out different reasons for different occasions, hoping one will click. In that respect, we're all passive quitters: we expect the reason itself to carry the burden, do it for us. Look at the pneumonia patient. He may even have been ultimately grateful for a circumstance beyond his control that gave him a good head start. He had no intention to quit: he suspended the habit because of necessity.

As long as we don't organize ourselves to succeed, we wind up by putting the blame on the latest reason in the latest attempt. Then it isn't we who have failed: the reason wasn't good enough to let us down. That makes us victims. Deprived of pleasure, we feel sorry for ourselves; we suffer. To relieve the suffering we turn back to an old ally which never lets us down: the habit. If this startles you, imagine yourself as a compulsive candy eater. The process of not quitting is exactly the same.

How to Combat Failure

At this point I recommend that you go back to Chapter four and study your list of reasons why you smoke. Remember how we'd discovered that most of the ways in which you use cigarettes are merely conditioned responses, connections to daily activities, only habits.

The real reason why we don't quit—why we cannot quit without proper preparation—is that we're so conditioned. The habit represents comfort and solace; rewards on big and little occasions; a buddy we can rely on; the only luxury we indulge. The "one more won't hurt" is the hedge.

So we're not just addicted to nicotine—we're mired in a habit, and we have to rationalize it.

Let's have some fun by substituting words. First, for "rationale" read "excuse" and you'll find that instead of addictive smokers we are addictive excuse finders. Sounds silly, doesn't it? If that's a habit, we definitely ought to break it. Then, substitute "routine" for habit. To break ourselves of anything implies an irreversible, imposed action, something we automatically resist. So instead of breaking a habit we now read,

Let's Change a Routine

Routines are part of our daily life. We follow any number of them, as they save us time and effort as we do our daily chores. We don't think about them until we get bored or until a different routine becomes more convenient. Think of any routine that you've changed now and then, such as the way you go to and from work, or how you organize your laundry day. For years you used to do the laundry on Mondays. Then something came up that could be done *only* on Mondays, something that made your life more interesting—a club meeting, a bridge party, a part-time job. So you moved the laundry to Tuesday. No problem. Or what about the Sunday-morning routine—whether to have a long bath or a leisurely breakfast first. When you felt there was an advantage in the new routine, it was a preference; it didn't require any will-power. In a previous chapter we called this rearranging priorities. It's more or less the same thing.

Willpower is an odd concept, one that is often both used and misused. Throughout this book I have tried to condition your mind toward a positive attitude, mostly in the way I've tried to use my own and other people's positive and forward-looking experiences to modify discouraging memories of struggles and failures. Stay with me while I explain the positive part in more detail.

The power of our will is the power of the "great human mind" which helps us to achieve the impossible. Sir Edmund Hillary used his willpower to reach the peak of Mount Everest, after his mind had convinced him that that was what he wanted to do more than anything else. Willpower works to support our mind, though it may cause some pain and hurt when we're trying to force it. In fact, no amount of willpower can make us do something that we don't really want to do. But as soon as our mind starts to meet willpower even halfway, the struggle begins to diminish. Let's play around with this for a minute, and then you can carry the exercise as far as you want.

"I don't want to go out in this weather and trudge to the office, but I have to." That's a completely negative statement and makes you miserable. Now modify the statement by using different reasons, somewhat as we did in Chapter five. "I don't want to go out in this weather, but I have to or I will lose my job, and I need the money." Now your reluctance is somewhat diminished because you have plans for the money.

Now see how a different reason begins to change the way you formulate that same thought. "I hate to go to the office in this weather, but we have the important meeting today," or even "but I'd rather go in today because I want to take Monday off." Your preferences are beginning to balance the negative and positive attitudes, and you have greatly reduced the willpower you need to make yourself go out.

Then compare that with "Normally I wouldn't want to go out in this weather, but we have theater tickets for tonight and have waited weeks to see the play." No lack of willpower here; in fact, it would take willpower to keep you at home.

You can compose dozens of sentences like that. You can also make a sentence that goes "I don't want to give up smoking but I have to or I'll die."

We've discussed that argument before and found it wasn't convincing enough because we all have to die sometime. It's just too negative. But see how the meaning changes, and your attitude too, if you add, ". . . before I've really lived," or ". . . before I see the children grown up," or whatever other wish you'd like a chance to fulfill.

What Can Make You Quit

It is my belief that you can free yourself of the smoking habit once you change the smoking routine by establishing other preferences for yourself.

Make the task easier. Establish a positive attitude for your reasons to quit—not as a form of self-denial or sacrifice, but as an exchange for something that's of greater value. That's an interesting twist, particularly when most smokers are used to thinking of quitting as giving up something they consider worthwhile.

Here's an amusing example of that sort of change in attitude —a true story. I was told of a. man who had been a heavy smoker but had stopped at a time when TV cigarette advertising was still allowed. He remarked, "I was getting more and more annoyed by the stupid cigarette commercials. One day, when I was watching a particularly inane situation, I decided I wasn't going to support that kind of stupidity anymore. I stubbed out my cigarette and haven't smoked since."

A cigarette commercial that made him quit smoking. Funny? But, of course, his mind had subconsciously concluded that there were better uses for his body, money, time. It doesn't matter how much or how little of the reason was clear to him at the moment. The main thing is that his mind had found a better way, and he needed no willpower to exchange something that was no longer worthwhile for something he wanted more.

Dr. Donald T. Fredrickson, a pioneer in the smoking-cessation effort and now a professor of public health at New York University, puts it into more scientific language. As a member of the New York City Board of Health, Dr. Fredrickson had the responsibility of providing citizens of New York City with a practical means of freeing themselves from the smoking habit. On the basis of his work at the clinics he had set up, he wrote his opinion of the key to lasting success: ". . . As we see it, there are two attitude postures one can opt for during withdrawal. One is negative and basically self-defeating. The other is positive and can be powerfully self-reinforcing.

"When the smoker opts for the self-defeating attitude, he tends to view withdrawal as an exercise in self-denial . . . that an object of great value is being taken from him . . . one that may be a source of pleasure. . . .

"When a smoker opts for the positive, self-reinforcing posture, he looks upon withdrawal as an exercise in self-mastery. Rather than taking something away, he is adding to his life a new dimension . . . bringing in turn a renewed sense of one's ability."

It happened to me. It's happened to many others. In fact, it is the very reason why I was determined to spread the word, first through the smokEnder program and now through this book. Not only is it possible to quit smoking without pain, but there is a mighty good chance that many other aspects of your life will be the better for it.

Here's one more example of how knowing your preferences can help you to stay an ex-smoker even when you're under stress. It happened to Barbara Davidson, now a fine moderator in our program, when she had not smoked for four years.

"One fall night," she says, "I checked in with my husband as I was leaving class. He reported that all was well at home and I said, in that case, I'd stop in at a neighbor's house on the way home to help plan the block association's annual children's Halloween party.

"About twenty minutes after I arrived at my neighbor's, I received a frightening phone call from my husband, who was at New York Hospital with our three-year-old boy. They were pumping out his stomach! He had found a bottle of Vicks Vapor Steam and had drunk it down. Camphor, the main ingredient, is highly poisonous. I dashed out of my friend's home and hailed a taxi, my heart pounding audibly. I screamed at the driver to get me to the hospital, that it was a matter of life and death.

"He responded to my panic by nervously lighting a cigarette and took off like a shot. I thought, 'I need one too. This is the worst thing that has ever happened to me.' Just as I was ready to ask the driver for a cigarette, I remembered what we had learned at smokEnders: smoking never makes anything better. What was it that I really wanted?

"1. I wanted the taxicab to go faster. Where had all this traffic come from?

"2. I wanted to be told that my son was going to be all right, that he would live and not suffer any permanent ill effects.

"3. I wanted to put my arms around my child and feel him breathing, hug and kiss him, and take him home.

"4. I wanted my husband to put his arms around me and tell me not to worry.

"It was very simple. Once I knew what I really wanted, I could see that it wasn't a cigarette."

When we hurt inside, it's an emotional discomfort. As smokers, we condition ourselves to believe that lighting up relieves us of even those things which weigh heavy on our hearts and minds.

It never does, of course. The problems are there long after the cigarette has been put out. It's important to try to articulate what you want. Once the real thoughts are permitted to take shape in your mind, you can see that you don't want a cigarette. You want the problem, the pain, a situation, fear, anger, hurt to go away. This is a good thing to know. It's like having a secret weapon.

BRIDGING THE GAP

You may remember that I told you in the Introduction that my main reason for writing it was to help you cross the span between deciding to quit and making it stick. If you don't remember, or if you didn't read the Introduction, go back to it now. It was my intention to start you off with all the good, positive and joyful lessons I learned and to share them with you. I've touched on them in almost every chapter, but now I'll put all the steps together.

1. Know yourself. Face up squarely to why you smoke, how much smoking really means to you and why you'd like to quit.

2. Don't be afraid it's too late. It was a turning point in my attitude when I came to realize, and could state with conviction, that my body would restore itself.

3. Learn to decide when you really want to quit and when you're only suspending the habit. That's very important. There's nothing wrong in itself with just suspending. At the very least, it will give your body a chance to recoup. Thousands of people give up smoking for Lent without too much trouble. They know it is only an interlude, and that knowledge sustains them. Once you have found you can stop for a limited time, you may find it easier to go the whole way. It's part of getting ready.

4. Once you really want to be serious, use the best reasons you've come up with to adapt your own attitudes. Set yourself a goal that's worth the trouble and then keep it in front of your mind. My favorite example of that is what I call the De Gaulle

method. As I remember hearing it, General Charles de Gaulle declared to his staff one day during the early years of the war, "I'm not going to smoke anymore," and being De Gaulle, he didn't. I don't remember whether we were told his reason, but it's conceivable that he finished the sentence "until France is free again." But regardless of whether it was a high ideal, sheer willpower or his ego that wouldn't allow him to back down, he suppressed his desire. No doubt he suffered from his craving, but he found other ways of refocusing his desire.

We ordinary people may not have quite such high ideals as the General's to sustain us. But you could make a bet with a friend, or pledge your word of honor to someone important to you. Whatever it is, use it to modify your attitude so that you can make your willpower work *with you* instead of *against you*.

5. In the smokEnder program, we spend considerable time training smokers in the art of distraction. Reshape and reorganize your habits by changing your rewards systems. Instead of reaching for a cigarette, reward yourself by "goofing off" for ten minutes and doing something completely different. Something you know you shouldn't be doing at the time but that gives you pleasure. It interrupts the pressure of the moment and reduces the need to smoke. Every cigarette you don't smoke is a step in the right direction. Every hour without a cigarette makes it easier to go without one for an hour and a half the next time.

6. Above all, learn to walk away from self-pity. Our most effective recommendation at smokEnders is to develop a sense of humor. Look at yourself the next time you feel self-pity starting to flow. As an amused parent would watch a loved child, smile at yourself and say, "That kind of feeling is kid stuff, and I'm grown up now. Self-pity is childish; it's not to be taken seriously anymore."

We found in our smokEnder program that a number of those who had previously failed had not fully understood the way self-pity works in us. They had paid scant attention to understanding themselves and weren't even aware that they had a habit of feeling sorry for themselves. But believe me, one of the biggest reasons why we smoke is because we need the recognition, reward and comfort that we've come to believe smoking stands in for. And the biggest reason we fail is that we have been conditioned to believe that giving up smoking is a form of saorifice. But we know better now!

These are really the basic points you need to observe in order to succeed. They are intensely practical; there's nothing mysterious about them. As I mentioned earlier, William James, the father of modern psychology, studied habit formation and came to recognize the essentials of making or breaking a habit. He wrapped it all up in a few sentences. You must first convince yourself that the new habit has value to you; then you must lay out a plan and practice it without exception. "Never suffer an exception," he said. And finally, once the new attitude is developed, you must never again "feed" the old habit.

fourteen

BENEFITS OF QUITTING

"What's in it for me?" you might ask, correctly. Perhaps you wonder if you're ready to confront quitting head on. It's a question of priorities. You've had a chance to look deeply into yourself, have discovered that you are the most important person in the world; you like yourself, and you care enough about your life to want to live it to your fullest potential. That's a good start.

Perhaps you were told you ought to quit smoking by your doctor. Perhaps a doctor or loved one even read you the riot act and said you had to quit smoking or else. Maybe that even scared you into a few weeks or months of abstinence and you went back as soon as the scare wore off, rebuilt your wall of rationalizations.

Have you ever quit smoking because you wanted to—from strong personal desire, pure and simple? Did you ever quit because the "want to" rather than the "have to" or "ought to" prevailed?

"Why should I want to?" Perhaps the burdens of smoking are becoming too numerous. The indignities, both physical and psychological, that you have sustained make you angry. Even better, perhaps the benefits are becoming irresistible. Graduates often tell me how amazed they are by the mighty accumulation of "pluses" they experienced when they quit smoking.

Here is a quiz to determine whether there's enough value in it for you finally to consider a serious attempt at quitting smoking. I have discovered in my work with smokers that the benefits can be broken down into three basic categories: Physical, Emotional and Social. Here are *one hundred and fifty* benefits. They were expressed by smokEnder graduates after just four weeks of not smoking.

Physical Benefits:

These statements are authentic; the names of the ex-smokers who made them are on file. They are real people, like you.

As you read the list, ask yourself if each item would be a benefit to you. To what degree? Circle the letter—A, B, C, D or E—that defines the degree.

I'm not going to include the most obvious benefits, such as "I've reduced my chances of getting lung cancer and heart disease . . . I won't suffer from emphysema . . . I'll never have Buerger's disease; I'll have good health" . . . Good health so you can do what? Live longer. Why? The benefits listed below are smaller and all concrete. They are about, as we so often say at smokEnders, the quality of life and the enhancement of ego.

A—Has no significance for me at all
B—Slight interest to me
C—It would be helpful
D—Sounds very good to me
E—Galvanizing!

Don't skip. It is important that you respond to each suggestion. Ask yourself, "Would I be happy to make that statement?" Then recheck the list and you'll see *your* reasons for wanting to quit. The A and B column will show you *what's in it for you* to quit smoking.

(CIRCLE ONE)

1. I never realized I could have so much energy.   A B C D E
2. My sense of smell has improved considerably.   A B C D E

3. I have a general feeling of well-being and feel more fit.   A B C D E

4. No short-windedness, and I'm breathing easier.   A B C D E

5. Mouth is no longer dry; tongue is no longer "brown."   A B C D E

6. Eyes are bright and clear, no longer bloodshot or puffy.   A B C D E

7. It's easy to ride my bike now—even up hills.   A B C D E

8. I can't believe it, but I'm no longer craving nicotine or climbing walls.   A B C D E

9. Sore throat is completely gone.   A B C D E

10. Smoker's cough is gone.   A B C D E

11. Breath smells fresh and clean and my mouth tastes better.   A B C D E

12. Find I have more time to do things.   A B C D E

13. Foods and drinks have sharper, clearer tastes.   A B C D E

14. Had a facial today—now maybe my face will stay cleaner.   A B C D E

15. Can breathe through my nose now instead of my mouth for the first time in years.   A B C D E

16. Nasal passages are free from burning and no longer congested.   A B C D E

17. My hair stays cleaner longer and doesn't stink of smoke.   A B C D E

18. Find I can climb stairs easily *and* talk at the same time; delighted not to have to stop at every landing to "admire the view."   A B C D E

19. Housework doesn't fatigue me anymore.   A B C D E

20. Beginning to feel alive again.   A B C D E

21. Don't feel "down" before I get up in the morning.   A B C D E

22. Fall asleep more easily and wake up refreshed.   A B C D E

23. No more heart palpitations.   A B C D E

24. Can swim better than in years—continuous laps, and even once across the pool underwater.   A B C D E

25. Feel calm.   A B C D E

26. No pain in my chest anymore—can even laugh at a joke without it hurting down there.   A B C D E

27. Played two sets of tennis and my legs finally tired before my wind ever did. A B C D E
28. I don't smell like stale smoke; I don't taste like stale smoke. A B C D E
29. More feeling in toes—went for a walk in freezing weather and my toes and fingertips didn't hurt from the cold. A B C D E
30. No more black sputum coming up. A B C D E
31. I no longer bulge in strange places from boxes of cigarettes stashed in various pockets. A B C D E
32. Don't have to sit in smelly smoking sections of movies, airplanes, commuter trains; have freedom of choice, rather than being "banished." A B C D E
33. House is definitely cleaner. A B C D E
34. No need to keep emptying ashtrays; saves time and energy. A B C D E
35. Acid indigestion is gone, and no more sour stomach. A B C D E
36. No more waking up in the middle of the night, and the attending "bladder condition" has disappeared. A B C D E
37. My skin looks alive, and the grayish-yellow pallor is gone. A B C D E
38. I enjoy looking younger and feeling younger. A B C D E
39. My hands no longer shake. A B C D E
40. No more black dots in front of my eyes. A B C D E
41. I'm dancing again—forgot how much fun it is. A B C D E
42. Began jogging daily—couldn't do this before for any period of time. A B C D E
43. Doing advanced yoga breathing daily. A B C D E
44. My walk seems to be more jaunty—purposely walking on sunny side of street so passersby can see how great I feel. A B C D E
45. I'm enjoying flavors and aroma I haven't experienced in years. A B C D E
46. I've cut down on coffee consumption—another addiction. A B C D E

47. No more of those late-afternoon headaches. A B C D E
48. Have more vitality during the day. A B C D E
49. Getting better at exercise; enjoying it more, too. A B C D E
50. Sex hasn't been this good in a long time! A B C D E

Social Benefits

51. I enjoy lots of good feedback from people I love. A B C D E
52. It's great to be able to make a point without waving a cigarette in your adversary's face. A B C D E
53. No longer have to scout for ashtrays upon entering someone's home. A B C D E
54. I enjoy not burning myself, my possessions, other people or their possessions. A B C D E
55. No more excuses for myself to my family, my physician, my boss or my friends. A B C D E
56. Glad to have eliminated a habit that today is considered socially offensive. A B C D E
57. Don't have to carry cigarettes during a party; two hands free—one for drink, one for hors d'oeuvres. A B C D E
58. Pleased with myself for being a trend setter— smoking is no longer "in." A B C D E
59. No longer late for appointments because of running back into the house to see if I "left one burning." A B C D E
60. My date didn't have to keep waving my smoke away all evening. A B C D E
61. Am appreciative of good cooking—no longer have to rush through the meal to light up. A B C D E
62. Was finally able to venture an opinion on some vintage wine without being told, "How would you know? Smokers can't taste anything." A B C D E
63. No longer will I make a fool out of myself cursing out delinquent cigarette-vending machines that "don't deliver." A B C D E
64. No longer so clumsy now that I have an extra hand. A B C D E

65. Didn't have to smell up my friend's apartment. A B C D E
66. Was able to break a child's fall without fear of singeing him. A B C D E
67. Easier to get close to people without having to worry about smoker's breath or smoker's odor. A B C D E
68. Was able to beat someone at tennis who is ten years younger than I am! A B C D E
69. Clothes smell fresh, stay cleaner longer. A B C D E
70. Feel at ease with people. A B C D E
71. Don't have to sit apart from people to accommodate my ashtray, smoke clouds, etc. A B C D E
72. Can enjoy theater without getting impatient for the intermission. A B C D E
73. Have been told I'm more "kissable." A B C D E
74. Fellow taxpayers and insurance-policy holders will not have to bear the financial brunt of my smoking-induced diseases. A B C D E
75. The social "crutch" is not needed anymore. A B C D E
76. I don't hide behind a cigarette. A B C D E
77. Sat through a really great movie, twice, and never thought of a cigarette. A B C D E
78. Cocktail before dinner no longer a trigger; nor wine with the meal. A B C D E
79. Never dreamed I'd be an inspiration to others. A B C D E
80. Didn't volunteer myself into a lot of "sorry situations" with great potential for self-pity, poor-me reactions. A B C D E
81. Feel more poised in social situations. A B C D E
82. Not reluctant about being physically close to others, as I think I smell good. A B C D E
83. No more anxiety about dropping ashes in other people's homes or begging for an ashtray. A B C D E
84. Believe it adds to my salesmanship not to have to subject customers to smoky room. A B C D E
85. I'm encouraging others to stop smoking; I guess that makes me a trend setter. A B C D E
86. Everyone around me seems delighted that I do

not smoke; one might say that I'm (you should
pardon the pun) de-lighted too!   A B C D E
87. Smoking is aesthetically ugly.   A B C D E
88. Am more talkative, not as shy.   A B C D E
89. No longer seen as an addict.   A B C D E
90. Don't have to excuse myself anymore to "run
    out" for a pack.   A B C D E
91. Don't have to fear burning loved ones or myself. A B C D E
92. I no longer impose my smoke on hapless victims. A B C D E
93. Feel more like everyone else now, sort of normal. A B C D E
94. Can concentrate on other people's conversation
    —I listen better without the distraction of a ciga-
    rette.   A B C D E
95. People don't complain or give me angry looks
    about polluting the air.   A B C D E
96. When I shop at the department store, I don't
    have to stand in that smoky, oppressive vestibule
    between the two sets of glass doors, finishing my
    cigarette on the way in . . . lighting up on the way
    out.   A B C D E
97. Love carrying a small evening purse . . . used to
    need a larger one to accomodate all my smoking
    paraphernalia.   A B C D E
98. Won't ever burn anyone else again in an eleva-
    tor.   A B C D E
99. Co-workers are so very supportive, and so many
    compliments on my success.   A B C D E
100. I'm no longer discriminated against.   A B C D E
101. Love life has definitely improved!   A B C D E

Emotional Benefits

102. I enjoy increased self-confidence.   A B C D E
103. I have tremendous feelings of accomplishment
     and pride.   A B C D E
104. It's great to be able to deal with stressful situa-
     tions calmly and maturely.   A B C D E
105. The "no concessions," can-do attitude is spread-

ing to other areas of my life.   A B C D E

106. Tremendous self-esteem which allows self-
     respect to return.   A B C D E

107. I love being able to "get to things" right away
     instead of wasting five or ten minutes finishing
     a cigarette.   A B C D E

108. Such great feelings that come from having done
     something positive and very special for me, my-
     self.   A B C D E

109. Wonderful not to need to buy cigarettes, not to
     have to carry them around, not to have to worry
     if I left them somewhere.   A B C D E

110. It's great to know that I can cope with anything
     now that I've quit smoking.   A B C D E

111. I enjoy having more money.   A B C D E

112. What a relief not to have to worry about starting
     a fire by accident.   A B C D E

113. Feel so proud of myself.   A B C D E

114. More in touch with my feelings.   A B C D E

115. Dealing with stress directly rather than resorting
     to cigarettes.   A B C D E

116. Sense of well-being permeating everything.   A B C D E

117. Able to eliminate self-pity instead of wallowing
     in it and smoking a lot.   A B C D E

118. I look in the mirror and see me smiling back.   A B C D E

119. I feel I've accomplished a fabulous task.   A B C D E

120. Happier, stronger, more relaxed and secure.   A B C D E

121. Don't need cigarettes to resolve my problems
     and/or conflicts.   A B C D E

122. I feel like a winner!   A B C D E

123. Sense of power and self-mastery.   A B C D E

124. I "shape up" and face situations, rather than
     erecting a smoke screen.   A B C D E

125. I guess I showed 'em!   A B C D E

126. No more guilt.   A B C D E

127. Beautiful sense of serenity.   A B C D E

128. I'm so happy!   A B C D E

129. My disposition seems to have improved; I smile
a lot more.   A B C D E
130. Looking forward to so many things; daring to
dream and plan again.   A B C D E
131. Don't need excuses anymore to leave the house
so I can smoke.   A B C D E
132. One less anxiety-producing thing to worry about
—panic is gone.   A B C D E
133. I've giving my positive emotions to people and to
rewarding activities rather than to cigarettes.   A B C D E
134. No longer have to make excuses for myself.   A B C D E
135. Peace of mind.   A B C D E
136. Sat in endless traffic, then waited in long line at
airport—both without that desire to smoke.   A B C D E
137. Gives me a feeling of getting a "new start" in
life.   A B C D E
138. I can say it: I don't smoke anymore!   A B C D E
139. Anxiety has changed into energy.   A B C D E
140. I don't have to be afraid anymore.   A B C D E
141. No longer have to make promises to myself that
I will quit smoking.   A B C D E
142. If I can quit smoking, I can do anything!   A B C D E
143. Support from family and friends is rewarding.   A B C D E
144. Feel like a celebrity—everyone asking me, How
did you do it?   A B C D E
145. New dignity.   A B C D E
146. Feel relaxed in "no smoking" areas where once
I would have felt personally threatened.   A B C D E
147. No longer have to make excuses to my children.   A B C D E
148. The hysteria has gone out of my life.   A B C D E
149. Petty things that used to bug me don't even get
a rise out of me anymore.   A B C D E
150. By quitting smoking I have proved to myself that
I do take responsibility for my own behavior—for
my own life. I'm no longer ashamed of me, but
proud of the new mature me!   A B C D E

SUMMING UP:
THINGS TO DO
IF YOU'RE READY TO QUIT

At this point you may be excited about the possibility of quitting and think there might be something in it for you. If that's so, you should do something about your increased motivation to stop. If you've followed the instructions and exercises in this book, you're very likely in gear to quit. Where do you begin?

I wish I could ensure your success by providing you with the smokEnders program right here and now. Unfortunately, it would be of little value to simply list the smokEnder techniques out of context of the seminar. The program is a highly structured 8 week seminar and builds on a number of crucial elements, such as your own personal involvement, accountability to someone each week, the play of dynamics among the entire group and most especially, the personal guidance and understanding of a trained Moderator.

Also, we've learned through years of experience not to try to explain the content of the smokEnder program outside of the seminar simply because our members tell us that an important factor in their success was the weekly element of suspense and surprise. Each week they returned eagerly anticipating their next instructions—wondering what new challenge would be presented. After quitting smoking, they generally agree that the not-knowing what was next had helped them stick with it. More important, they weren't tempted to skip steps or accelerate the process. Should you someday choose to quit by attending a smokEnder seminar, you'll understand this concept.

To date, our only means of presenting the method effectively is in the seminar framework. We hope that someday we'll be able to teach it by even more accessible means. I wish we could put it into capsules or tablets and distribute them throughout the country as a sort of mass inoculation to help all smokers who want to quit. That would be about 90 percent of all smokers, according to a recent report by the U.S. Department of Health, Education and Welfare.*

The smokEnder method is an easy way to quit, provided it is set in the proper structure and presented in the correct sequence, as it is in our seminars throughout the country and in several foreign countries. I gained the expertise that led to it through years of trial and error and researching every quit-smoking book I could get my hands on. So while I wish I could give you the magic words in book form, I am a firm believer in a structured class program.

It may be, however, that you are a different type of smoker than I was and can do-it-yourself with the instructions that follow.

As I have emphasized all throughout this book, I have come to believe fervently that the single most important element in successful quitting is preparation and the attitude one brings to the enterprise. So until and unless you decide to enter a smokEnders seminar, my recommendation is to take advantage of your now highly developed desire to quit, together with your new confidence in your real ability to stop smoking, and consider the following action:

First, let's review what you've found out about smokers in general, and about yourself as a smoker, and then I'll offer you some techniques which may be helpful on a do-it-yourself basis.

---

*". . . 9 out of 10 smokers have either tried to quit smoking or would probably do so if there were an easy way to do it."—*Adult Use of Tobacco*, 1976.

____You very likely have discovered that you really would like to quit smoking. You are probably disgusted with the habit for a lot more reasons than you had when you started reading this book. There's no question you'd exchange the habit for freedom from all the nuisance and problems. You can't seem to justify smoking to yourself any longer.

____You have sorted out the reasons you started to smoke as a youngster and found they had nothing to do with your current reasons for continuing to smoke.

____You accept the fact that nicotine is addictive—and you're very likely rather pleased to learn as a result that your willpower is not in question. You've learned that nicotine is generally out of your system within three or four days, and you are prepared to deal with that as a transient problem.

____You've thought about the physical dangers of smoking (everything from fires to lung cancer) and you've realized how dependent you are upon your cigarettes.

____You've become aware of all the other habits that attached themselves to your smoking habit, like coffee, cola, alcohol, and you don't like having been shoved into doing things you can't easily control.

____You've also recognized how much of an automaton you've become by reaching for a cigarette whenever you get a signal or cue, such as the ringing of the telephone or clink of the coffee cup. Most likely you resent being outer-directed instead of inner-directed.

____You've learned about the power of the cigarette ads on your psyche and your consumer nerve. You'll soon be truly immune to the ads, but in the meantime you're defusing their power by satirizing them.

____The idea of quitting as tangible evidence of your self-mastery has great appeal. You're toying with the possibility that quitting smoking may also be an exhilarating experience.

____You now understand the relationship between smoking and weight gain and know that you don't necessarily gain weight because you quit—and you won't use that excuse as a cop-out for not quitting.

___You've learned that you're not alone. Hundreds of thousands of smokers felt the way you do at this point. They couldn't imagine themselves not smoking. And they couldn't believe they could ever quit. But they did. And you can too.

___You've begun to imagine yourself as a nonsmoker. You should now develop a mind-set in which smoking is an impediment to your desires.

___You have stopped telling yourself, "I enjoy smoking"; instead, you acknowledge the fact that you're generally rather disgusted with the habit and wish you could quit.

___You've begun to sell yourself on the idea of quitting as a positive experience—and to persuade yourself that you really *want* to quit.

___You've learned techniques for dealing with situations and acquired tools to cope with life without using your cigarette as an amulet and cure-all. You've analyzed your own personal use of cigarettes and reasons for smoking, and you discovered it isn't the cigarette that gets things done or protects you. You've realized it's *you* and your own ability, personality, intelligence that are responsible for your success. You have begun to suspect you might even be more able without the impediment of a cigarette to slow you down or drug your mind.

___You've learned that smoking doesn't make anything better. It doesn't make bad news better or fix broken objects, for instance.

___You understand now why smoking doesn't calm you down or steady your nerves. In fact, you realize that smoking, plus coffee, tea or cola, makes you more nervous and jittery.

___You've learned that those rationalizations we all use to protect the habit are downright silly. It would be difficult for you ever again to use one of those excuses without feeling foolish. And as an added support, you will laugh when you hear other smokers make the same statements and use the same phrases you used to.

____And most of all, you've learned that you must treat yourself with respect. You must convince yourself you're worth every effort. And in order to show that respect, you will reward yourself frequently, set worthy goals for your talents and ambitions, not allow yourself the childishness of self-pity or martyrdom and choose to live your life by your own command, instead of the cigarette's. You have decided that smoking will no longer dominate your existence. You want to be your own person.

If you're able to check off most of those statements as ones you agree with, then you should jump right into the next stage of planning for quitting. You should make up your mind that you're going to stop once and for all. Remember, there is no right or wrong way to quit. Whatever works for you is what counts. And there is no right or wrong time to quit, either. If you wait until your life smooths out, you'll never quit.

Here, then, are some certain central techniques which are useful outside the framework of a control program:

1. You might want to call a friend to do it with you, but be certain his or her interest in quitting is at a peak. If you are a very private person, you might want to go it alone and keep a diary of your progress and your plans.

2. Now set a timetable for yourself. In the smokEnders program we work on an eight-week schedule. Several weeks of smoking as you prepare to quit, and then several weeks of support and reinforcement to learn how to handle situations as a nonsmoker. (For instance, many smokers say they're afraid they won't know what to do with their hands after they stop smoking. We assure them it will be no problem, but make light of it by saying, "You wash them, dry them, fold them and put them away.")

So set a date a couple of weeks from now as the big day. Pick a date that doesn't coincide with a visit from your mother-in-law or exam week. Circle that day and date on all your calendars. It should be sacred. *Nothing* should interfere with it. Don't consider changing it. You might want to announce the date to all your friends and co-workers, but I suggest you work at this quietly and privately. What you don't need is outside pressure. In addition, I've learned that one of the serious obstacles to quitting is the malice of some smoking friends. If they learn of your quitting attempts, they become alarmed and, perhaps from subconscious motives, offer you cigarettes—blow smoke in your face—tease you for being "chicken" and afraid of cancer. (Your best weapon against their sabotage is understanding. They are afraid they'll be the last smoker in the office or car pool or bridge club.)

3. During the time between now and your big date, begin to condition yourself physically and emotionally for the big event.

a. On pages 103–104 are three steps to lower nicotine in your system. They're worth repeating here:

i. Step up your circulation by additional exercise. Jumping Jacks are the next-best thing to swimming for maximum results. I suggest you begin a regimen of increased exercise daily, with doctor's okay if you have any physical problems.

ii. Begin drinking water regularly. Clear, cold water when you get up and before you go to sleep, and several times during the day. It not only increases circulation, which in turn adds oxygen to your blood; it also improves your bowel functioning and digestive system, helps flush your kidneys and by cleansing the poisons out of your system more rapidly, makes you feel better. Now, there's a miracle drug.

iii. You can reduce the amount of nicotine by changing brands, but this is dicey unless you're really going to stop within a very short time, because you'll smoke more to get the "right" amount of nicotine.

b. Build your mind and body to the healthiest level possible. Plenty of rest. Light, nourishing meals. Avoid fatigue.

c. In addition to increasing your intake of water, begin to drink milk and juice as much as possible. And reduce your alcohol intake as much as possible, for now. A good trick that we suggest in the smokEnders program for those people who feel obliged to order a cocktail or highball at a party or business lunch is to water it down, using more mixer than before.

4. Analyze which cigarettes each day you enjoy and which you do not. Until your quit time, become fully conscious of each cigarette you light up. Make a pact with yourself that you'll smoke only those you really want. In that way, you'll likely eliminate a good number each day with no effort or self-denial. (Remember, if you're still enjoying more than two, you may not be ready to stop.) When you're about to light up ask yourself, "Do I really want this cigarette, or am I only lighting it automatically?" If the answer is that it's automatic, put off lighting it up for a while—say, an hour. Or until the next checkpoint in your day, such as lunch break. You should notice a gradual reduction in the number of cigarettes you buy each day. And you should now buy only by the pack. No more cartons. Because it helps if you change your brand repeatedly. Break the "old buddy" syndrome while you're at it. No more brand loyalty. Try not to smoke two packs of the same brand in a row. Another good technique for making yourself aware of each cigarette is to use the opposite hand or put cigarettes in an unfamiliar location or different pocket so that you break the automatic "reach."

5. Consider collecting all your cigarette butts in one large container. There's no better way for you to see the actual filth smoking represents. "Tar" becomes real and visible instead of just an advertising word.

6. Cut down on coffee, tea and cola. This not only reduces your jittery "coffee nerves" but also eliminates one of the things you associate with smoking.

7. Meanwhile, begin to develop strong personal reasons for wanting to quit. Reasons that will offer you benefits beyond self-preservation and obligation. One of my most powerful reasons (not the most powerful—that was extremely personal) was that I didn't want to become a little-old-lady smoker. I hate the look of it. So you see, good reasons may not have anything to do with your health. Motivation is the key to your success. Find reasons that are meaningful to you. Not intellectual reasons. Gut reasons. Ego reasons.

8. Begin to plan for the time when you don't smoke anymore. Think of ways to reward yourself with the money you will have saved. Calculate it and plan to spend it on something for yourself. In the smokEnder program, we require our members to repay themselves for the program tuition with the money they saved by not smoking. Then we insist they save up to buy themselves something entirely frivolous. After all, you used to burn it up— now you can use it for anything you'd like and not feel guilty spending it.

9. Before your big quitting date, if you're concerned about weight gain, put yourself on a simple, efficient weight-loss program for a few weeks. Then, if you should happen to gain, it won't become an excuse to start smoking again.

10. Do something to develop and maintain a clean mouth taste.

11. Before you reach your big day, do a dry run. Walk your way through it as a nonsmoker. Experience it in your mind and then, when you actually live it, you will have already absorbed the shock.

12. When the big day arrives, smoke your last cigarette and say with finality and conviction, "That's it. *I don't smoke anymore.*" And don't tease yourself with the possibility of having one now and then. That leaves the door open to an option which lets the thought of having a cigarette enter your mind. And once in your mind, it gets stuck there until you either cave in and have one— or sell yourself over again on the strength of your intention to break free.

I assure you, the important attitude at this juncture is to view quitting as an addition to your personality and well-being, rather than something you have given up. Then, if the thought of a cigarette comes to mind, you will have a ready mind-set: "Not me: *I don't smoke anymore!*"

After the big day comes, you will need a few weeks to get used to not-smoking and to being a nonsmoker. It's almost unreal, since you probably don't know what it's like to be an adult nonsmoker. As your body shifts gears and changes occur, you must be on the alert for conditions that might otherwise cause you to panic, such as changes in your body and natural functions. For instance, there is a substantial number of reports of postcessation swelling and related weight gain caused by fluid retention. It isn't cause for alarm, and it usually disappears within a few days, but forewarned is forearmed.

Don't be surprised at any new conditions that occur shortly after quiitting. If they persist, or alarm you, by all means see your doctor for reassurance. Be certain to tell him you have just quit smoking. He will no doubt explain the reasons in terms of body chemistry.

Because these changes are so common, and represent the body's ability to restore itself, smokEnders call these conditions "Symptoms of Recovery." Our members rejoice if they have evidence of their bodies' being able to repair themselves.

13. So if you become constipated or develop diarrhea, or your gums bleed, or your tongue becomes sore, don't be alarmed. These are ordinary changes and are very transient. Be happy that your body is still healthy enough to repair itself. Don't use the temporary inconveniences as an excuse to give in to a more inconvenient habit—smoking!

14. And after you've quit, never forget what it took to break free. It wasn't a cinch. It could well be one of the most significant actions you have ever taken on your own behalf. So don't risk losing your freedom. There are many subtle traps ahead. The most insidious is classic: "One won't hurt." Well, take it from the many case records of smokers who have quit successfully and comfortably—and to their surprise, resumed smoking because they felt they had it made and that "one wouldn't hurt."

We say in the smokEnder program: One will hurt! So until you're stabilized in your new habit of not-smoking, put another sign in your mirror and on your desk that says, "One will hurt." If your resolve begins to falter and you consider taking a cigarette, declare to yourself: *"It's not negotiable. I have no options. I've quit."*

15. To increase your motivation to stay quit, you must constantly reinforce yourself for the first few months. Therefore, as you discover new reasons why you're glad you quit, write those reasons on little cards—one per card—and put them in highly visible places: on the mirror in your bathroom, on the windshield of your car, on your desk, and so on. Be on the constant lookout for added reasons why you enjoy not-smoking.

There are many subtle reasons which will emerge over a long period of time if you keep alert for them. For instance, many months after I quit smoking, I realized my eyelids didn't burn when I awoke in the morning. It used to be so difficult to open my eyes—my eyelids felt like sandpaper. When I quit smoking, the scratchiness disappeared. Coincidence? No. Apparently the smoke had caused a chronic sub-clinical irritation.

Another discovery after I quit smoking: For years when our children were young I'd sing to them and accompany myself on the guitar. When our oldest child, Joan, became big enough to manage a guitar, we sang and played together frequently. Even as a small child she had a good ear and a lovely voice. It was a pleasure we all enjoyed. But our little concerts became shorter and shorter because my throat began to pain me after a short round of singing. I suppose deep down I suspected a relationship between the pain and my smoking, but I didn't mention it. How could I indict my beloved buddy? By that time, my family had begun their campaign to get me to quit smoking. So I made excuses, and Joan sang without me. After a few years I stopped singing altogether. Joan went on to become the family songmistress; but we had all loved to sing when we were together, and I regretted no longer being able to take part. It was a pleasure denied. Looking back, I think it was probably my first truly personal reason for wanting to quit smoking. The discovery, years later, that I could sing without discomfort—and, as a bonus, that my voice became clearer and not so deep—was a strongly reinforcing surprise reason.

Don't take not-smoking for granted. Reinforce yourself. But *you* must look for reasons why you're glad you don't smoke anymore.

16. For a while after you have stopped smoking, develop a clean, fresh nonsmoking environment around yourself. Surround yourself with nonsmokers. Find a spot in your office where the air is fresh and see if you can have your desk moved. (Remember, Donna Shimp insisted, and Ma Bell—AT&T—was obliged to provide her with a nonsmoky area.)

17. Another trap for many ex-smokers is self-pity. If you should happen to feel sorry for yourself for any reason—don't reach for a cigarette. Laugh at yourself for being childish, and say to yourself, *"Smoking won't make anything better.* What is it I really want?"

18. After you quit, don't abuse your friends with your self-righteousness or hassle them about their smoking. Rather, tell them how well you feel now that you don't smoke anymore. It's very reinforcing to tell others how much energy and vitality you now feel. For instance, it's more helpful to yourself and your smoking friend to say, "Since I quit smoking I can jog a couple of miles" or "play two more sets of tennis before wearing down" or "run up the stairs without becoming winded." Your friends will applaud you instead of avoiding you. And you might save a life, because your friend might take interest in quitting because you made it seem so desirable and pleasurable.

And you can reinforce yourself by creating a local nonsmoking epidemic among your friends, business associates, colleagues, relatives. Your example will certainly infect others. People will say, "If you could quit smoking, I can." Encourage people to quit for the *pleasure* of not-smoking. It's a strange new concept. And it's real.

19. Finally, each month, on your anniversary of quitting, plan a really fine celebration. Take yourself out to dinner, to the thea-

ter or to a sporting event—or buy yourself something special on that date. It will become as important and remembered as your birthday—and in fact, it might well be. For many of us, it is the day we really began to live as free people.

LAST WORD

Thousands of letters and completed questionnaires from smok-Ender Graduates are receivd each week. Typically, they celebrate the act of quitting and the joy of not-smoking. Smoking is a great equalizer. Quitting is too! Following are a few comments by Graduates which show the diversity in age, occupation and smoking history of smokEnder Members. You can identify with someone who perhaps has smoked as long as you have, or as many packs per day, or has a pressured and demanding position or profession.

Data from the hundreds of thousands of in-depth questionnaires returned by Graduates are utilized by universities and others for research in such a way as to preserve the anonymity of our Members. The following people have given permission for their names to be used in this book. (The date following each quotation is the date on which the Member stopped smoking.)

"I am prouder of having stopped smoking than of almost anything else I have accomplished in the last ten years. I will be forever grateful to smokEnders."—*Barry Manilow, singer-composer. (4/30/76)*

"I think it's a wonderful program. I think it is sensitive and scientific. It's wonderful to feel that someone cares and doesn't condemn your weakness, and at the same time can offer such constructive help, and if the person wants to stop smoking I see no way that it can fail. I offer my heartfelt thanks to God, to smokEnders and to dear Addie [Addie Gerber, smokEnders Moderator] for helping me as they have."—*Rosemary Harris, actress. (2/25/76)*

"SmokEnders [quitting smoking] has been the most incredible thing I have ever done for me and me alone. Everything else in a full lifetime had revolved around my husband and chldren; this is the one thing that has been completely mine."—*Gertrude Eltman, Long Island City, New York, who had smoked between 3 and 4 packs a day for almost 40 years. (7/11/75)*

"I enjoy life more and like myself more."—*J. Messina, Meriden, Connecticut, who had smoked 2 packs a day for 21 years. (2/20/74)*

"I'm now able to run between one and two miles every day—and feel great afterward! Before, ever since I had started to smoke, I couldn't run a hundred yards."—*William Verschuren, Chatham Township, New Jersey, who had smoked 2 to 3 packs a day for over 14 years. (2/24/77)*

"I've said it over and over, but I will never stop saying it—thank you so much. I couldn't have done it without you. And not to miss it!! Improvements noticed since quitting: Clean teeth. Great skin color and texture. Hair, too. Altogether much more life."—*Tamara Daniel, actress, New York City. (2/22/74)*

"I have truly come to enjoy *not* smoking."—*Melvin Kushner, D.D.S., Owings Mills, Maryland, who had smoked 1 1/2 packs a day for 19 years. (6/11/76)*

"I have more energy—do not tire as quickly as before while doing anything physical. I feel marvelous. Have no desire to begin smoking again."—*Barbara Goldberg, Flushing, New York, who had smoked 1 1/2 packs a day for 25 years. (5/1/74)*

"I feel fantastic. Am glad I came into contact with smokEnders at a young age. After previous unsuccessful attempts to quit, smokEnders was easy."—*John M. Doherty, M.D., Aston, Pa., who had smoked 1 pack a day for 11 years. (3/3/76)*

"I smoked for 40–45 years, tried every way known to man to quit and finally went to smokEnders as a last resort, with little hope of success. I'm still amazed and delighted to be completely free of the desire for a cigarette."—*Alfred Bloomingdale, Los Angeles, California, founder of Diners Club. (7/15/76)*

"SmokEnders is fantastic! It offers a remarkable program to help people quit smoking—calmly, comfortably and permanently. I am personally thankful for smokEnders. I am thankful for our profession because for the first time we can send the patient who must stop smoking to the one organization that is most likely to help him succeed."—*I. Norton Brotman, D.D.S., F.A.C.D., Clinical Professor of Oral Diagnosis, Dental School, University of Maryland. (10/24/75)*

"I have never been happier over stopping something. I feel so much better, I breathe better, my complexion is better, and those cancer commercials no longer bother me."—*Al Malone, St. Petersburg, Florida, who had smoked 1 pack a day for 42 years. (2/26/77)*

"I am more calm and feel better than I have in years. I even have my beverages without thinking of a cigarette. There is no question my self-image has improved, and I am forever grateful to smok-Enders."—*Joan Hillenbrand, Batesville, Indiana, who had smoked 1 1/2 packs a day for 25 years. (10/28/76)*

"We can never fully believe we quit smoking so easily. Smoking was something we did continuously. It seemed unlikely that either or both of us could quit. Many thanks."—*Mr. and Mrs. James Durham, Astoria, Oregon. (1969)*

"The program provided a number of insights and techniques which I have found valuable in remaining cut off."—*A. R. Hutson, Summit, New Jersey, who had smoked a pack a day for 30 years. (2/27/74)*

"Exhilaration is the only word I can think of to adequately describe the feeling of quitting smoking by the smokEnder method. It's the best life investment I have ever made."—*Ross Reid, Executive Director, Consulting Engineers of Ontario, Toronto, Canada. (10/29/76))*

Lil's X-rcise

create YOUR OWN PROGRAM! Only requirement: Make it FUN! As long or as short as you like... You'll stick to it if its yours. Include something from each group. Love ♡ your body !! !! 6 !!! !! 5 times a week?!

I. Warm-ups
stretches, bouncy & rhythmic with move music. Breathe conciously. Begin thinking sweet thoughts.

A. Standing
B. Sitting
C. Lying
D. Inverted

Do bounces, swings, kicks, and stretches in each position...

II. Strength
(No guilt, no negativity. Every move you make is progress. Forget the flab.)

These exercises give you the most workout in the shortest time. Do as many/few as you wish.

A Sit-Ups (any style)
B Pushups (regular or knee bent)
C Tilt

Feel which muscles are being used: feel them tense & relax.

D. Leg Lifts (raise & lower slowly)

E. Prone Arch (raise trunk & legs high!)

III. Creative Dance
Listen and move to your favorite music. Think about rhythm, tempo (fast and slow), mood.

IV. Stamina
(cardio-vascular)

Jumping jacks (or jogging in place, hara dancing, jumping rope). Check with your doctor.

1st-2nd week . . . . . 2½ minutes
3rd-4th wk . . . . . 5 minutes
5th week . . . . . 7 minutes
6th week . . . . . 10 minutes

V. Breathing & Relaxation
Slow, controlled, deep breathing (yoga-style). Awareness of conciousness & how you feel. Good! Sit or lie down.

Love Lilla

COMPARE

THE COST OF MAINTAINING A CAR

1 GALLON OF GAS — 60¢ — 1 PACK OF CIGARETTES

THE COST OF MAINTAINING A SMOKING HABIT

In addition to the cost of cigarettes – there is a hidden cost of smoking. . . . A MAINTENANCE CHARGE! The average smoker incurs additional costs to maintain the smoking habit, just as he incurs maintenance costs on his car. Consider that the cigarettes are like the gasoline. It costs a lot more to maintain your car or your smoking habit, than just the gasoline or the cigarettes. Your figures may be different from the averages shown below, and some items may not apply to you at all; so we've provided a column for you to figure out your own cost of maintenance.

ALL FIGURES ARE APPROXIMATE FOR THE PURPOSE OF THIS EXAMPLE

INSERT YOUR OWN FIGURES IN THIS COLUMN AND COMPUTE

INSURANCE	$ 200	DOWN TIME DUE TO SMOKING ILLNESS (5 days average)
ACCIDENTS (MINOR)	100	AUTO SCRAPES DUE TO SMOKING ($100 deductible)
	50	BURNED CLOTHING DUE TO SMOKING
	75	BURNED CARPETS AND FURNITURE
OIL	100	FLINTS, BREATH MINTS, MOUTH WASH, COLOGNES, NICOBAN, LIGHTERS
ROUTINE REPAIRS	35	ADDITIONAL DENTAL CARE (20%)
	60	ADDITIONAL MEDICAL TREATMENT & PRESCRIPTIONS
GENERAL MAINTENANCE	115	EXTRA DRY CLEANING; CLOTHING, DRAPES, etc.
PARKING, WASH & WAX	150	MORE FREQUENT HOUSE, CAR & OFFICE CLEANING MORE CLEANING COMPOUNDS, AIR SPRAYS, WEAR & TEAR
GARAGING	110	REPAINTING HOME/OFFICE MORE FREQUENTLY
FINES, TICKETS AND TOLLS	20	INTEREST AT 6% (not compounded!)
MISC	50	MISC: EXTRA MILEAGE TO RUN TO THE STORE FOR A PACK; HIGHER INSURANCE PREMIUM (about 5%), TAKING TAXI INSTEAD OF BUS IN ORDER TO SMOKE.

PER YEAR **$1065.** AVERAGE — $_____ YOUR COST

NOW ADD THE COST OF CIGARETTES TO CALCULATE THE COST

PER MONTH **$ 90.** AVERAGE — $_____ YOUR COST

© SMOKENDERS® Inc., Phillipsburg, New Jersey 08865 1975 (Rev. 6/77)

ACCORDING TO A RECENT SURVEY OF SMOKERS CONDUCTED BY THE CENTER FOR THE STUDY OF SMOKING BEHAVIOUR.

Jacquelyn Rogers' Method

SMOKENDERS®
"The Easy Way to Quit Smoking™"

COST OF SMOKING CHART

CALCULATE THE COST OF CIGARETTES:

AMOUNT SAVED PER DAY	PER DAY	PER WEEK	PER MONTH (30 DAYS)	PER YEAR (365 Days)	10 YEARS	AMOUNT SAVED DURING PROGRAM AFTER CUT-OFF	PLUS MAINTEN-ANCE COST (See Over)	TOTAL AMOUNT SAVED DURING PROGRAM
55¢ per pack								
1	$ .55	$ 3.85	$ 16.50	$ 200.75	$ 2,007.50			
1½	.82	5.74	24.60	299.30	2,993.00			
2	1.10	7.70	33.00	401.50	4,015.00			
2½	1.37	9.59	41.10	500.05	5,000.50			
3	1.65	11.55	49.50	602.25	6,022.50			
3½	1.92	13.44	57.60	700.80	7,008.00			
4	2.20	15.40	66.00	803.00	8,030.00			
4½	2.47	17.29	74.10	901.55	9,015.50			
5	2.75	19.25	82.50	1,003.75	10,037.50			
65¢ per pack								
1	.65	4.55	19.50	237.25	2,372.50			
1½	.97	6.79	29.10	354.05	3,540.50			
2	1.30	9.10	39.00	474.50	4,745.00			
2½	1.62	11.34	48.60	591.30	5,913.00			
3	1.95	13.65	58.50	711.75	7,117.50			
3½	2.27	15.89	68.10	828.55	8,285.50			
4	2.60	18.20	78.00	949.00	9,490.00			
4½	2.92	20.44	87.60	1,065.20	10,658.00			
5	3.25	22.75	97.50	1,186.25	11,862.50			

75¢ per pack				
1	.75	5.25	22.50	273.75	2,737.50
1½	1.13	7.91	33.90	412.45	4,124.50
2	1.50	10.50	45.00	547.50	5,475.00
2½	1.88	13.16	56.40	686.20	6,862.00
3	2.25	15.75	67.50	821.25	8,212.50
3½	2.63	18.41	78.90	959.95	9,599.50
4	3.00	21.00	90.00	1,095.00	10,950.00
4½	3.38	23.66	101.40	1,233.70	12,337.00
5	3.75	26.25	112.50	1,368.75	13,687.50
PLUS COST OF MAINTAINING THE HABIT:	$3.00 per day	$21.00 per week	$ 90.00 per month	$1,095.00 per year	$10,950.00 per 10 years

$ _ _ _ _ _ + $90.00 = $ _ _ _ _ _

REWARD YOURSELF...DO SOMETHING NICE FOR YOURSELF. SMOKING IS ACTUALLY PUNISHMENT IN THE DISGUISE OF REWARD SO, REWARD YOURSELF WITH SOMETHING PLEASANT.

Instead of burning this money, consider spending it on tangible pleasures and objects--completely frivolous or very serious...for YOURSELF!

First you might want to repay yourself for this program. You've made an investment in yourself which will pay off better than any other investment you've ever made. PERSONAL FREEDOM AND IMPROVED QUALITY OF LIFE.

Then write some ideas of items you would like but have 'begrudged' yourself over the years. Trips, books, sports equipment, hobby items--anything within the range of your savings.

© smokEnders, Inc., Phillipsburg, New Jersey 08865   1969 (7 Rev. 6/76)   Printed in U.S.A.   (Blue) Cost of Smoking Chart P/M/115